Draw Basic Lines

Trace the lines from ●→ to ●.

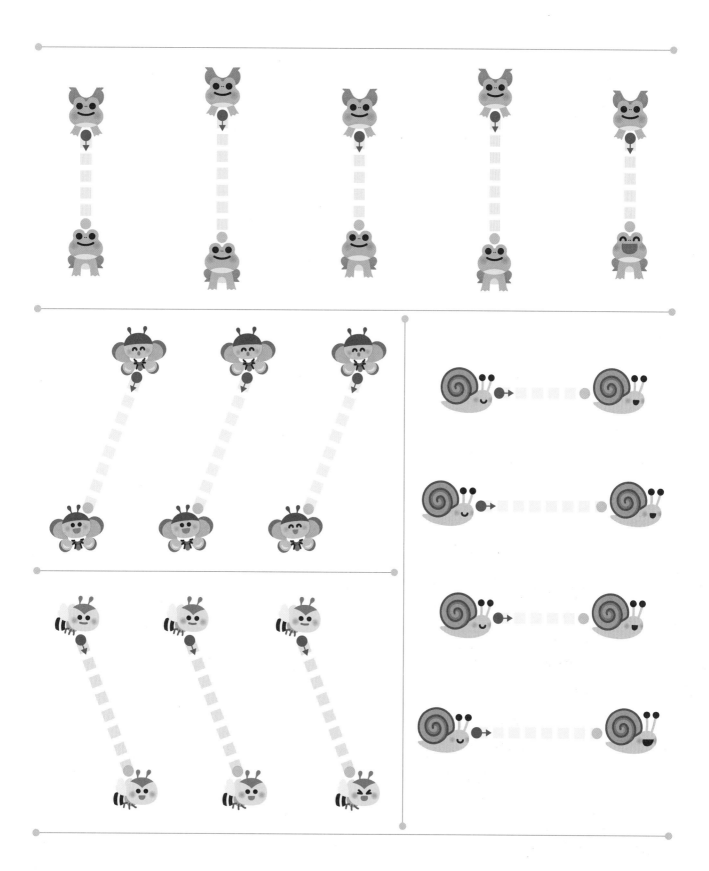

Trace the lines from ●→ to ●.

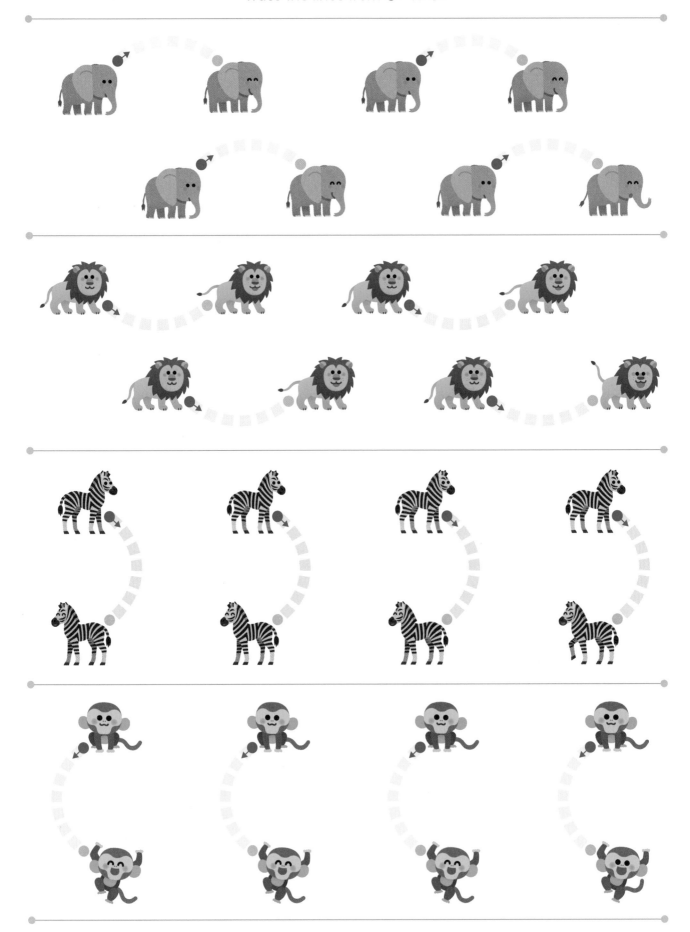

BASIC LINES

Trace the lines from ● to ●.

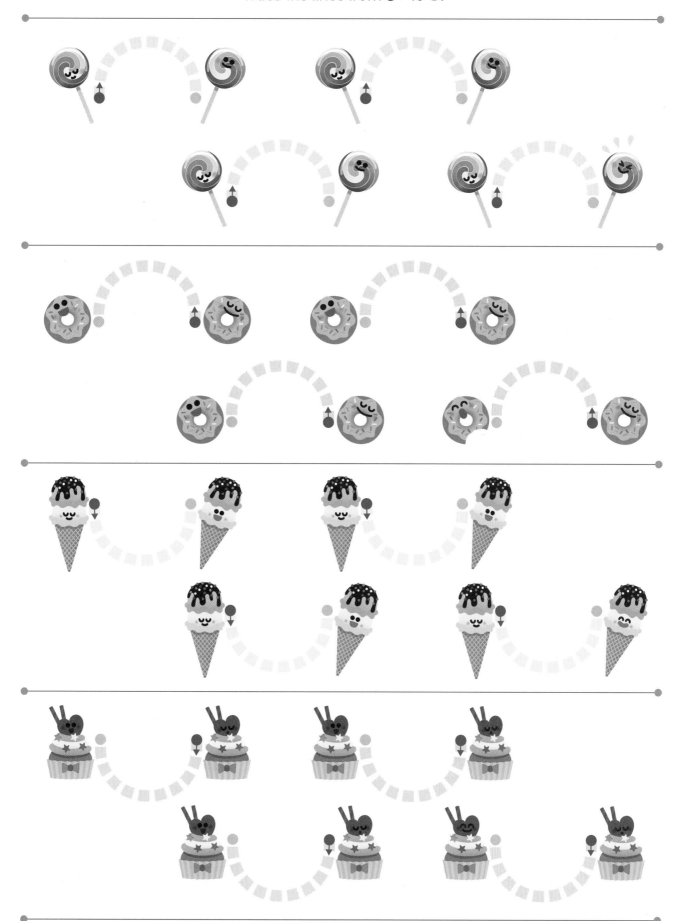

Trace the lines from ●→ to ●.

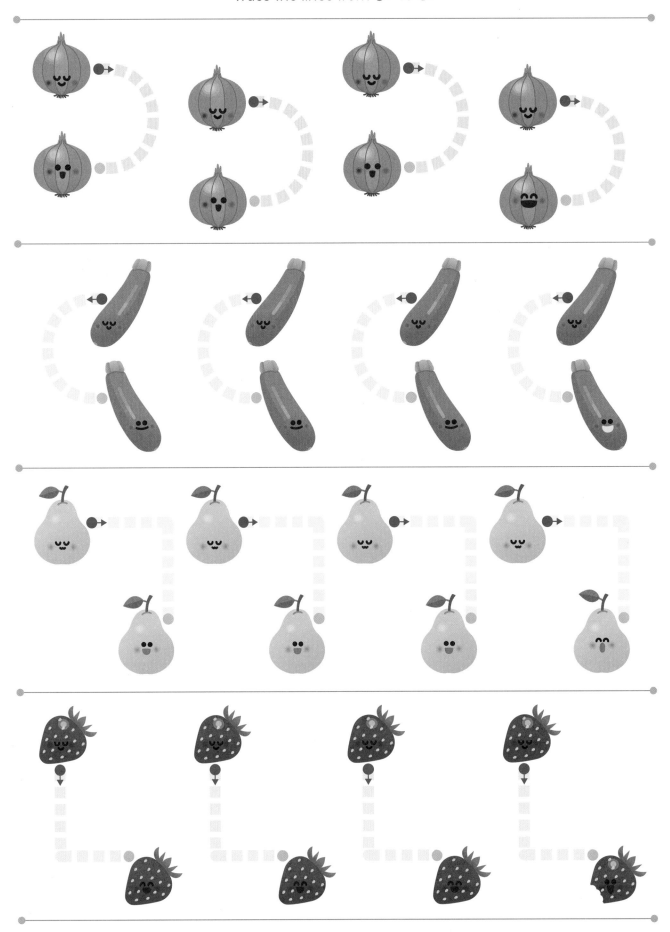

BASIC LINES

Trace the lines from ●➙ to ●.

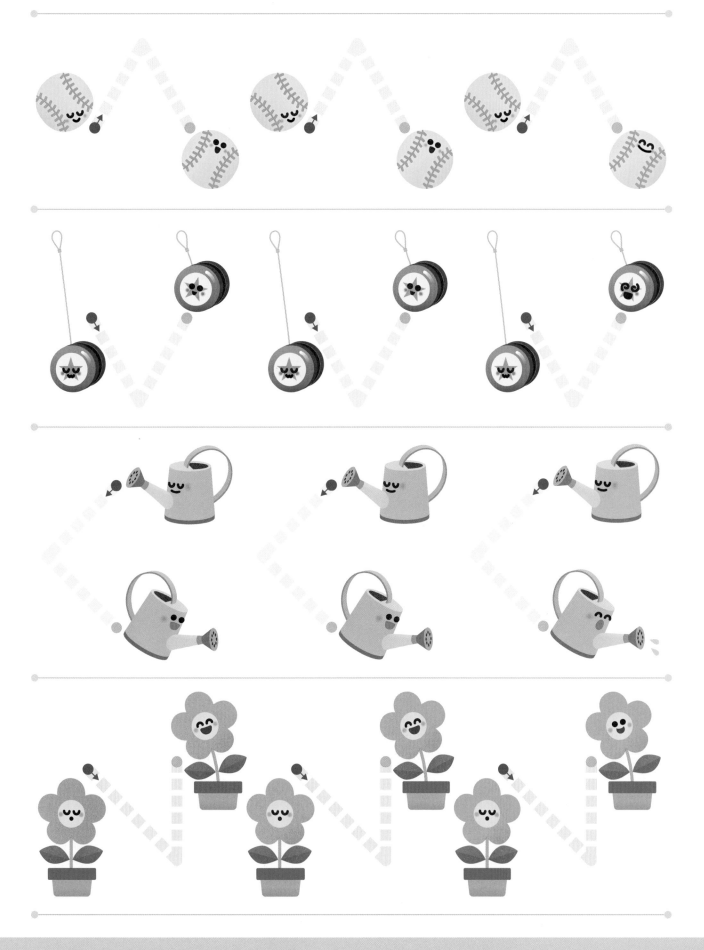

Trace the lines from ● to ●.

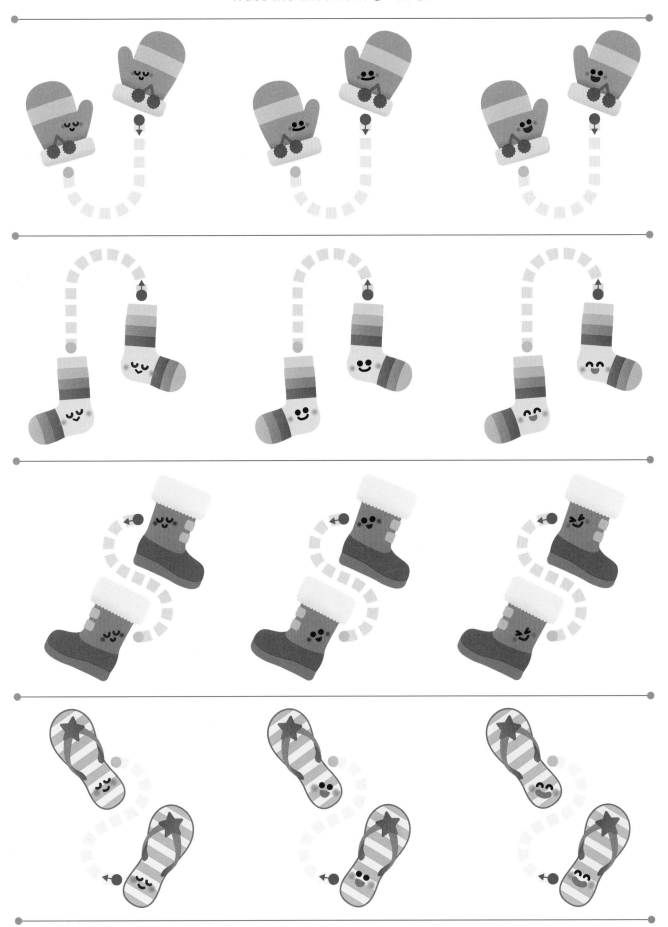

BASIC LINES

Trace the lines from ● to ●.

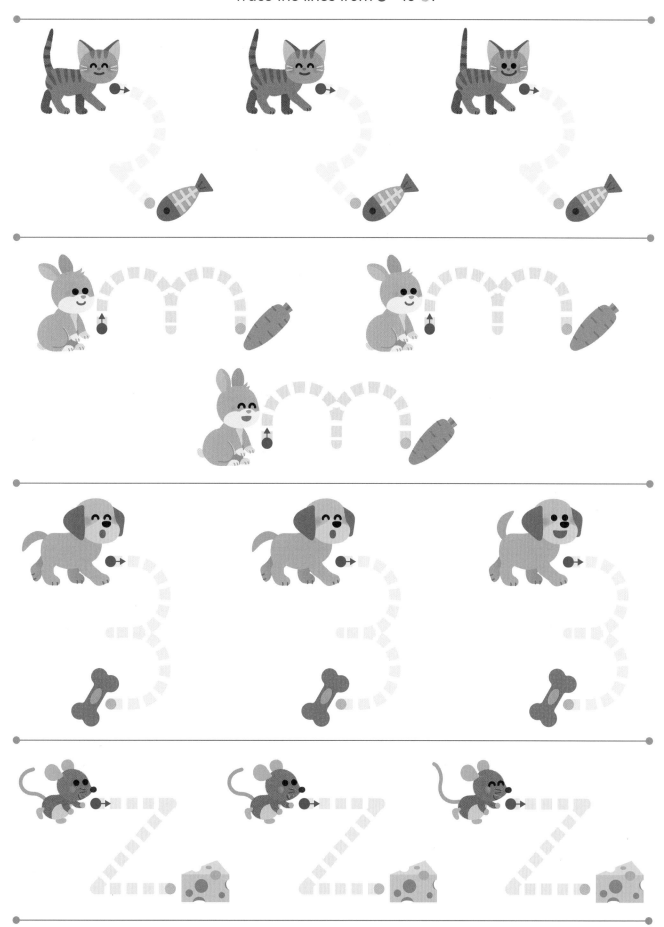

Trace the lines from 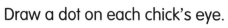 to ●.

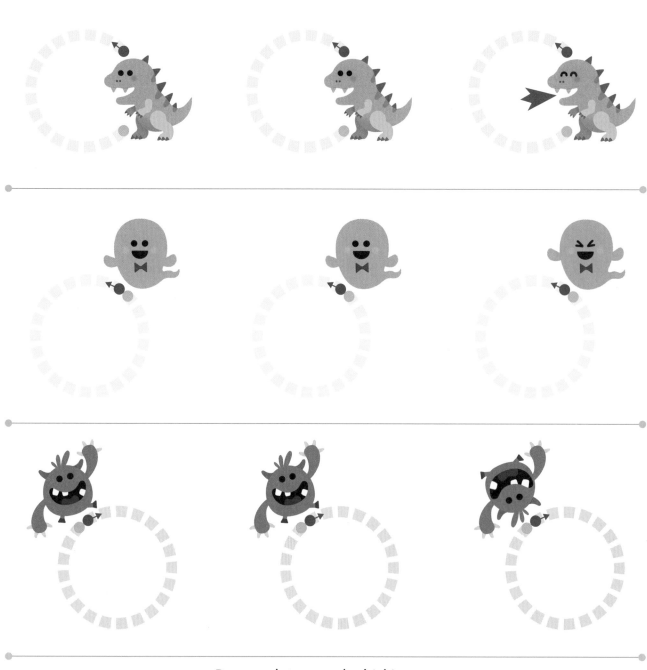

Draw a dot on each chick's eye.

BASIC LINES

Trace the lines from ●→ to ●.

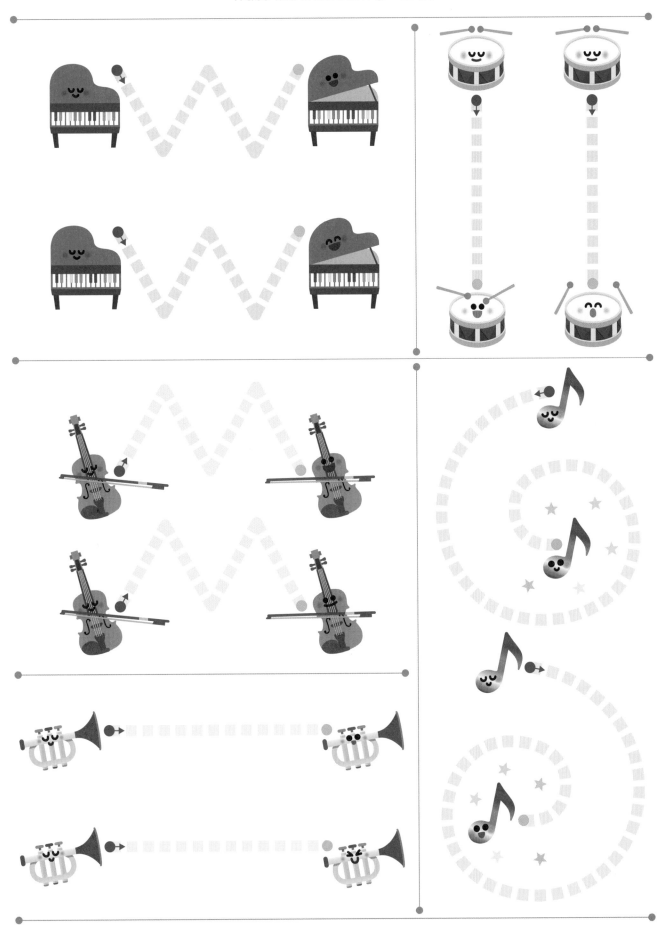

Trace the lines from ●→ to ●.

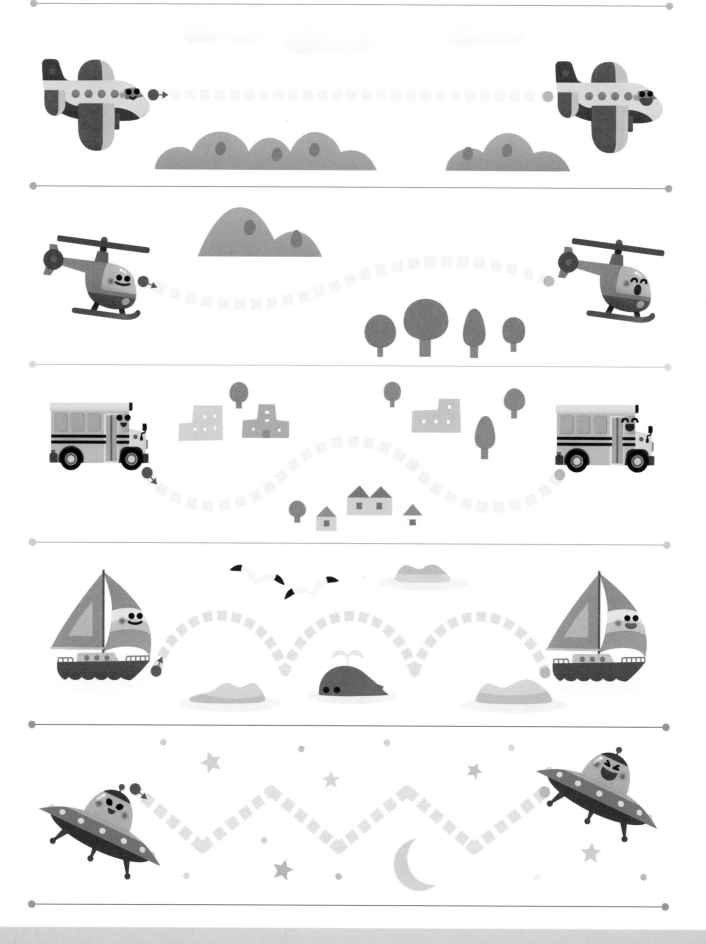

BASIC LINES

Trace the shapes and say each name.

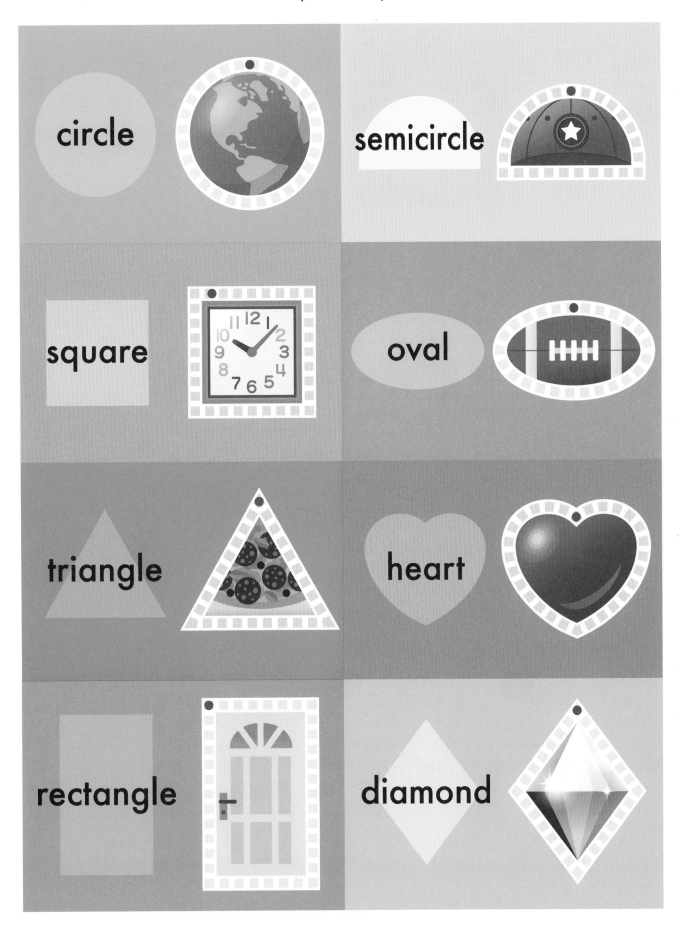

circle

semicircle

square

oval

triangle

heart

rectangle

diamond

Trace the circles.

Draw a line from ➡ to ➡.

circle

Trace the squares.

square

Draw a line from ➡ to ➡.

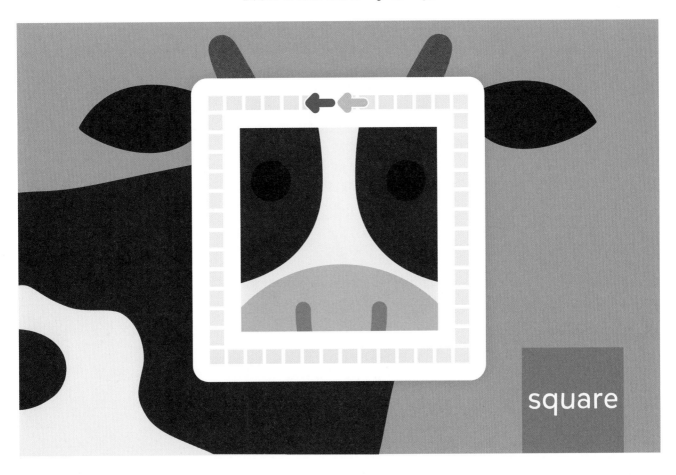

square

Trace the triangles.

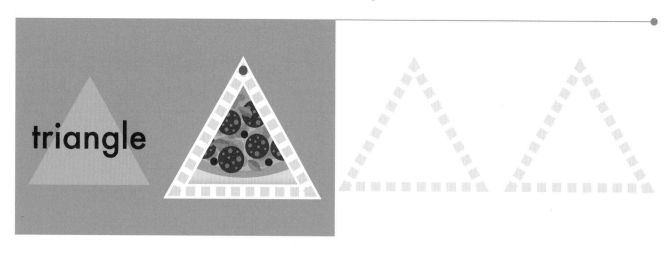

triangle

Draw a line from ➡ to ➡.

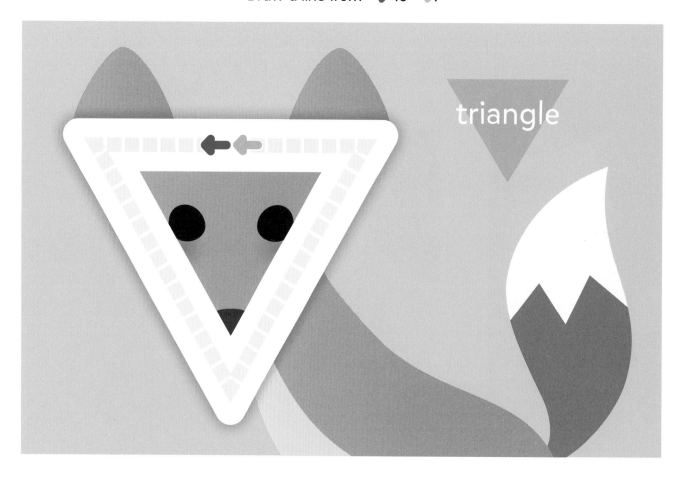

triangle

Trace the rectangles.

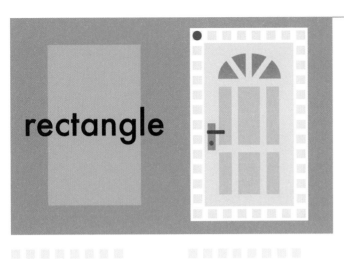

rectangle

Draw a line from ➡ to ➡.

rectangle

Trace the semicircles.

semicircle

Draw a line from ➡ to ➡.

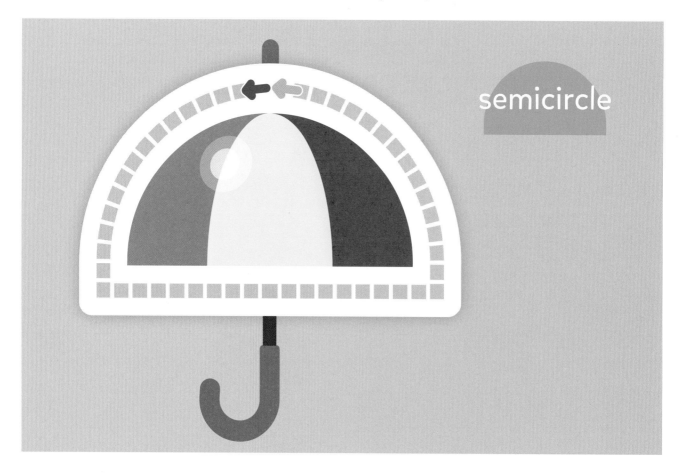

semicircle

SHAPES

Trace the ovals.

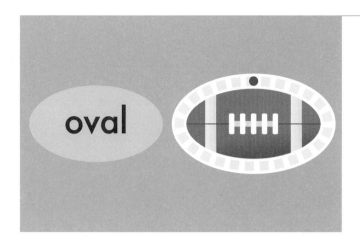

Draw a line from ➡ to ➡.

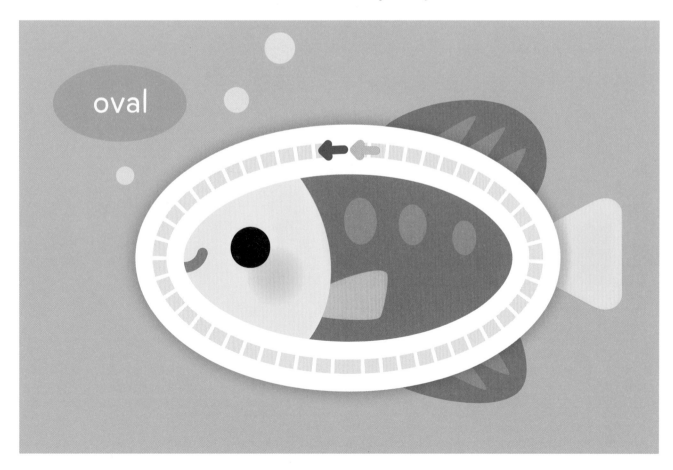

Trace the hearts.

heart

Draw a line from ➡ to ➡.

heart

SHAPES

Trace the diamonds.

Draw a line from ➡ to ➡.

Find and Trace the Shapes

Find the shapes in the picture. Then, trace the shapes from ➡ to ➡.

Find and Trace the Shapes

Find the shapes in the picture. Then, trace the shapes from ➡ to ➡.

Connect the Shapes

Draw a line to connect each shape to its matching shape in the picture.

example

square

diamond

heart

circle

Connect the Shapes

Draw a line to connect each shape to its matching shape in the picture.

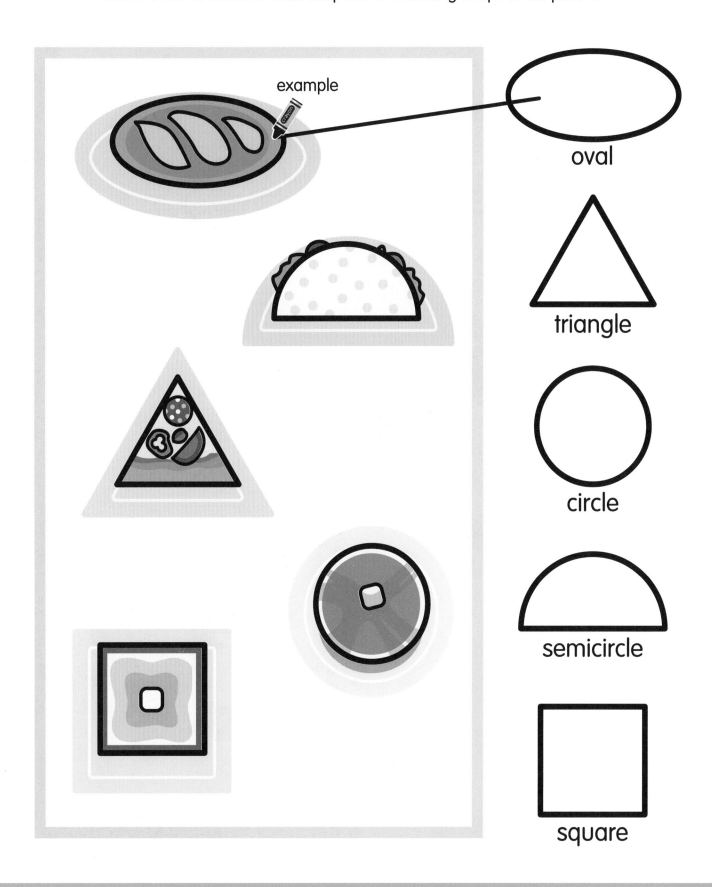

example

oval

triangle

circle

semicircle

square

Color the objects red. Then, say their names.

red

fire engine

strawberry

apple

tomato

ladybug

crab

red

COLORS

Color the objects orange. Then, say their names.

orange

orange

pumpkin

basketball

carrot

fox

orange

Color the objects yellow. Then, say their names.

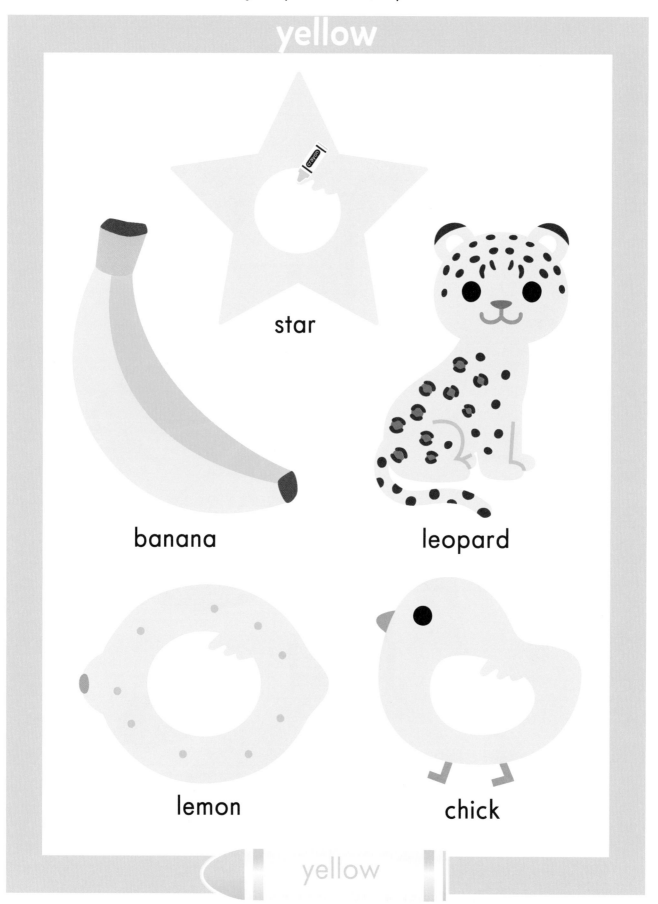

star

banana

leopard

lemon

chick

yellow

Color the objects green. Then, say their names.

green

leaf

zucchini

tree

alligator

frog

green

Color the objects blue. Then, say their names.

blue

sky

balloon

fish

sea

bucket

blue

Color the objects purple. Then, say their names.

purple

eggplant

grapes

plum

pansy

purple

Color the objects brown. Then, say their names.

brown

boot

chair

monkey

horse

nut

brown

Color the objects black. Then, say their names.

black

umbrella

crow

sunglasses

piano

black

apple

airplane

alligator

ant

Color the apple.

A is for apple.

Trace the lines from ➡ to ➡.

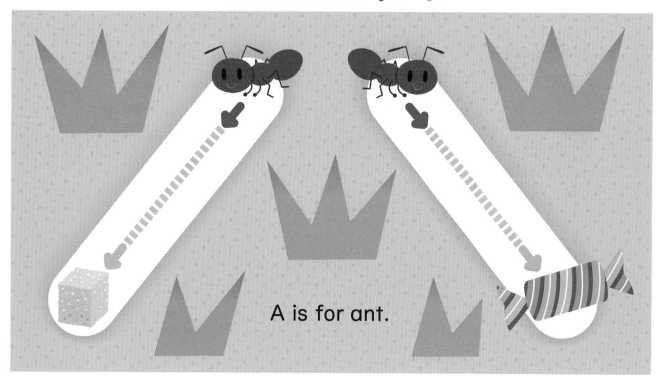

A is for ant.

Trace each letter.

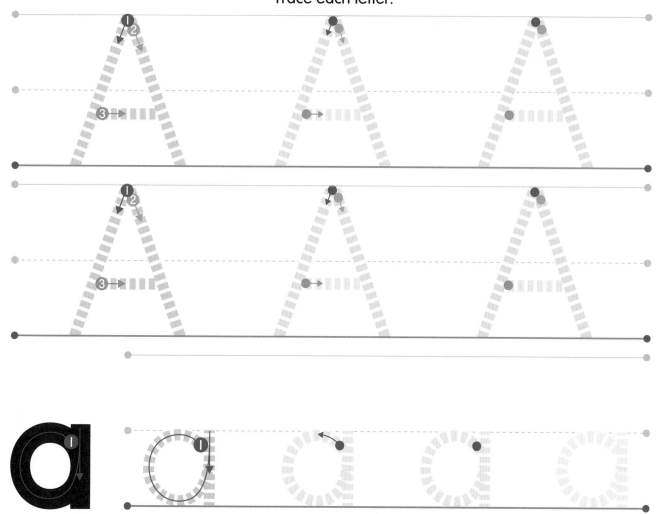

bear

bee

banana

ball

Color the banana.

B is for banana.

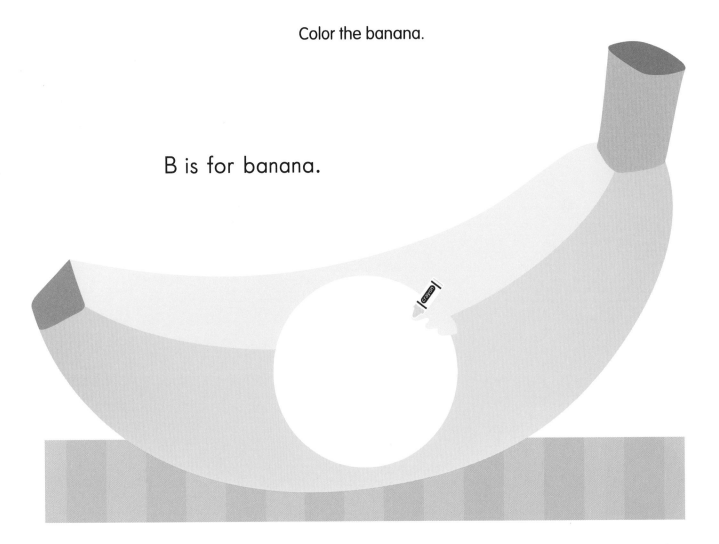

Trace the lines from ➡ to ➡.

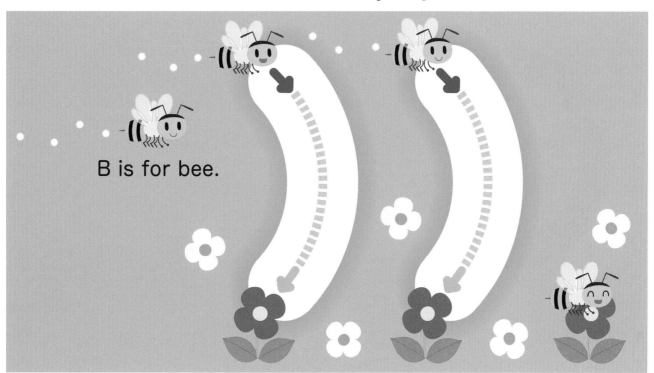

B is for bee.

Trace each letter.

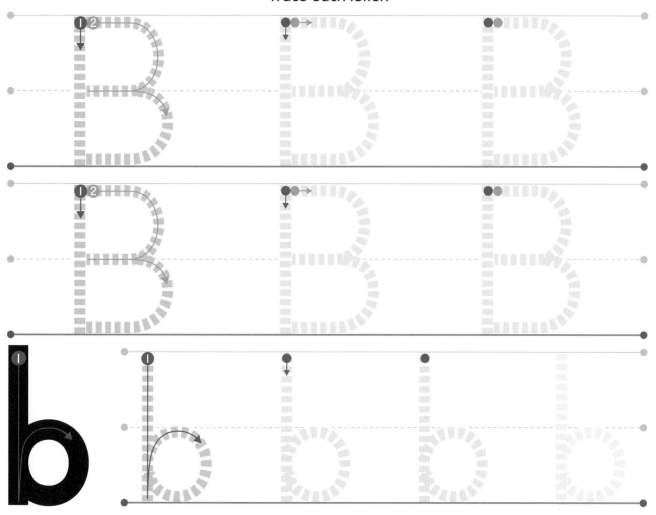

cat

cake

carrot

car

Color the carrots.

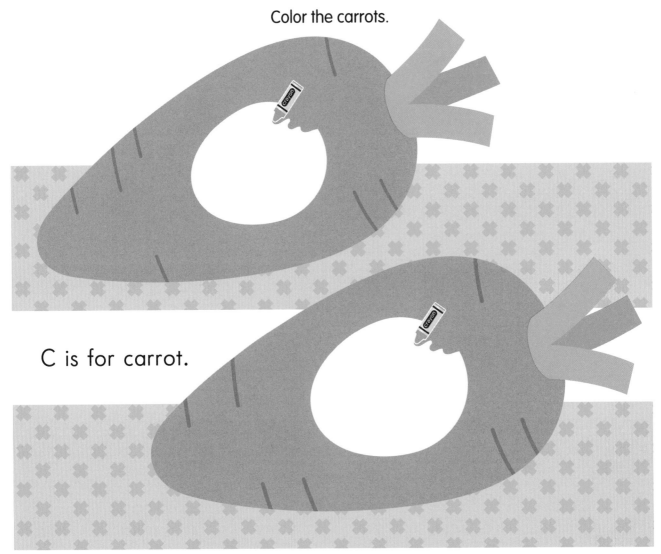

C is for carrot.

Trace the lines from ➡ to ➡.

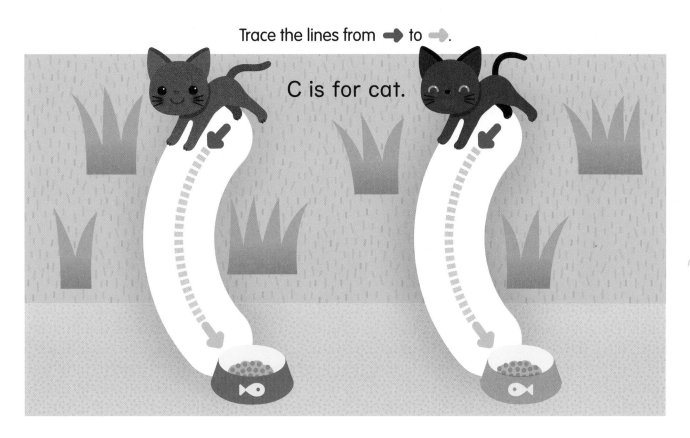

C is for cat.

Trace each letter.

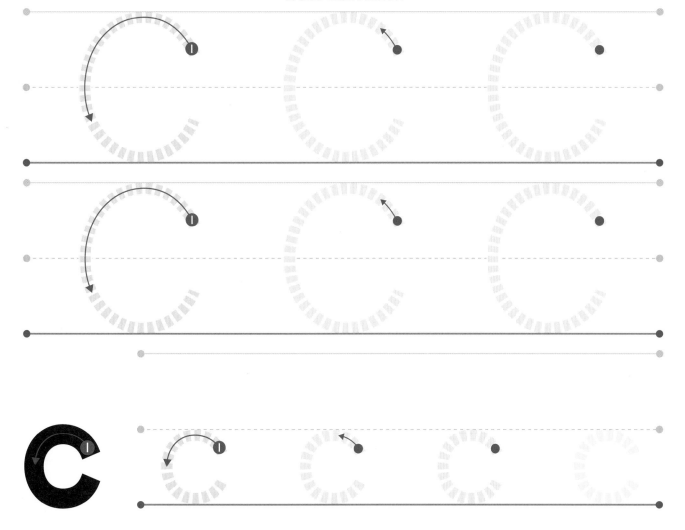

D

dog **d**uck

doughnut **d**rum

Color the dolphin.

D is for dolphin.

Trace the lines from ➡ to ➡.

D is for duck.

Trace each letter.

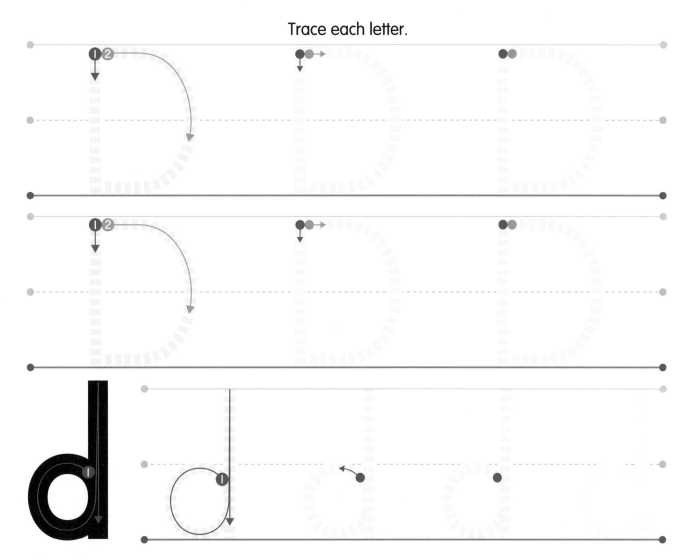

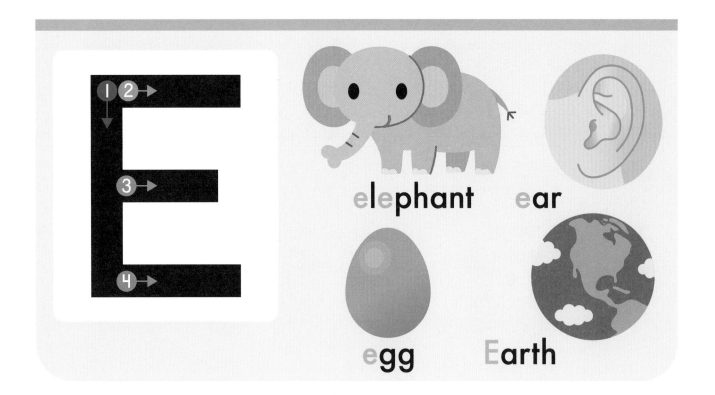

elephant ear

egg Earth

Color the elephant.

E is for elephant.

Trace the lines from ➡ to ➡.

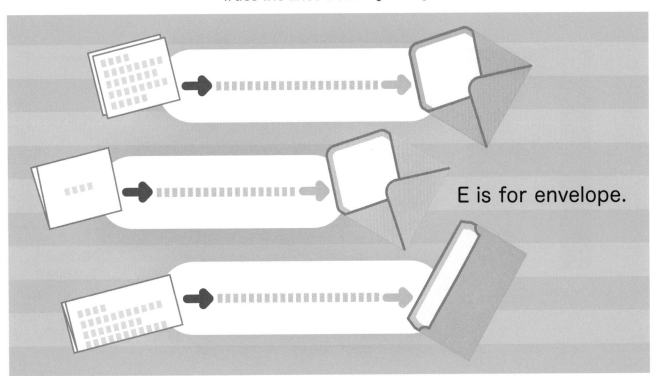

E is for envelope.

Trace each letter.

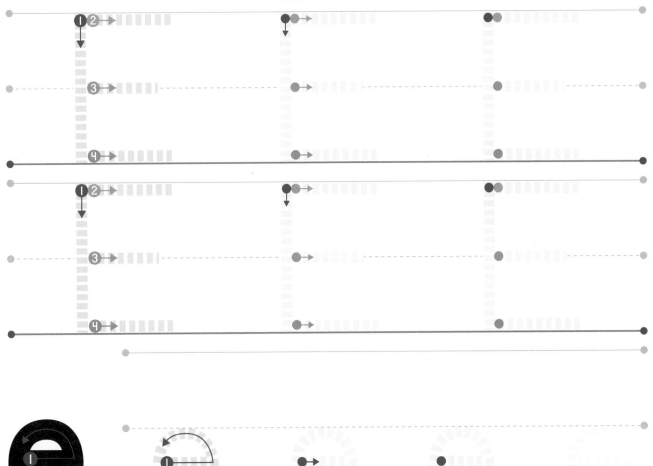

fish

flower

frog

fire engine

Color the flowers.

F is for flower.

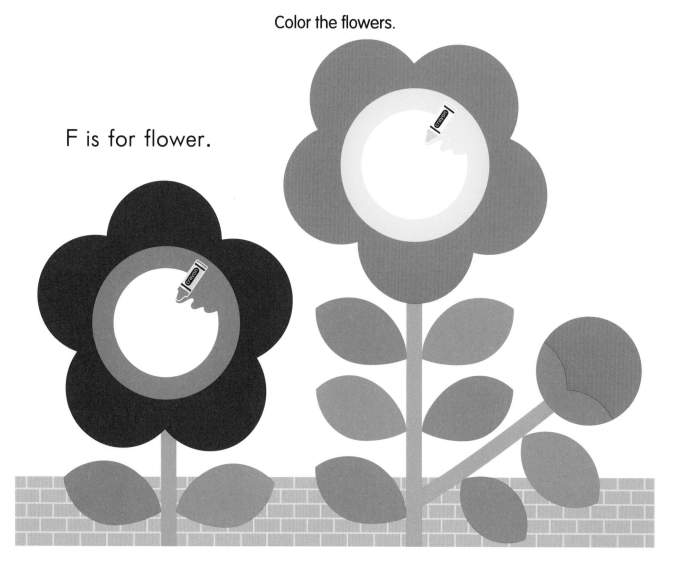

Trace the lines from ➡ to ➡.

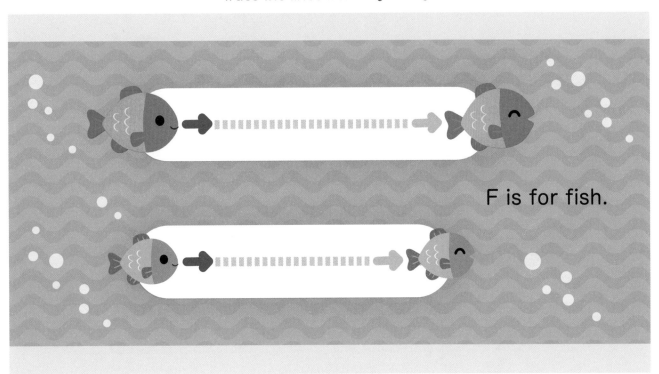

F is for fish.

Trace each letter.

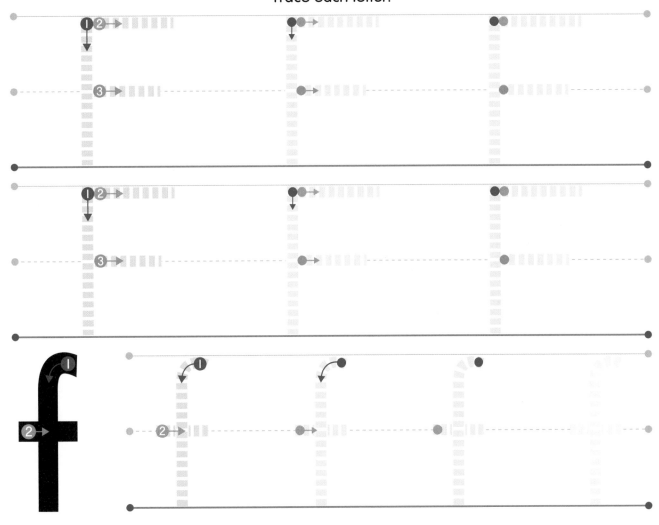

giraffe

grapes

glasses

guitar

Color the grapes.

G is for grapes.

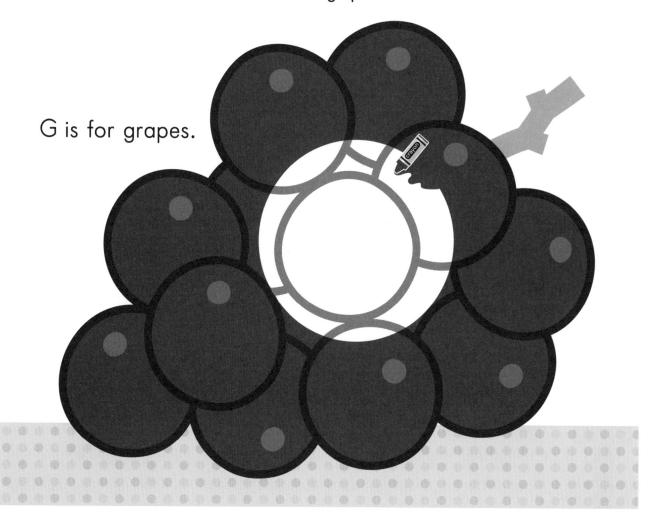

Trace the lines from ➡ to ➡.

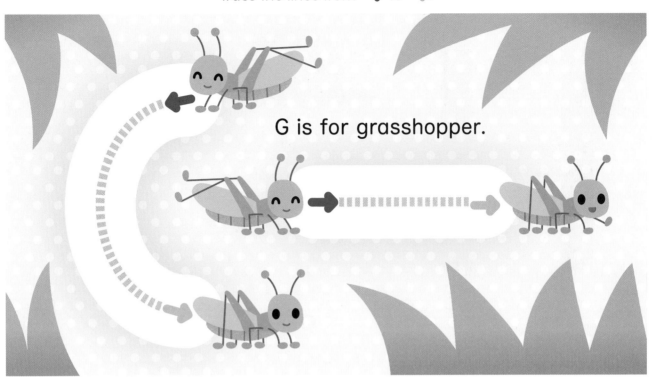

G is for grasshopper.

Trace each letter.

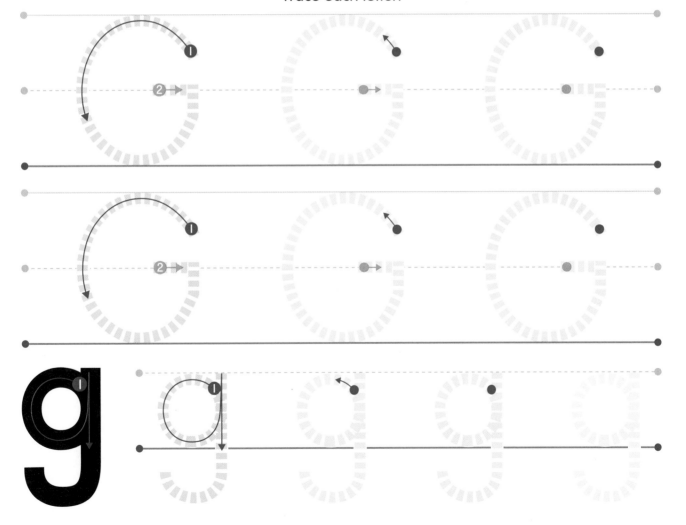

h at

hedgehog

h orse

h and

Color the hearts.

H is for heart.

Trace the lines from ➡ to ➡.

H is for hat.

Trace each letter.

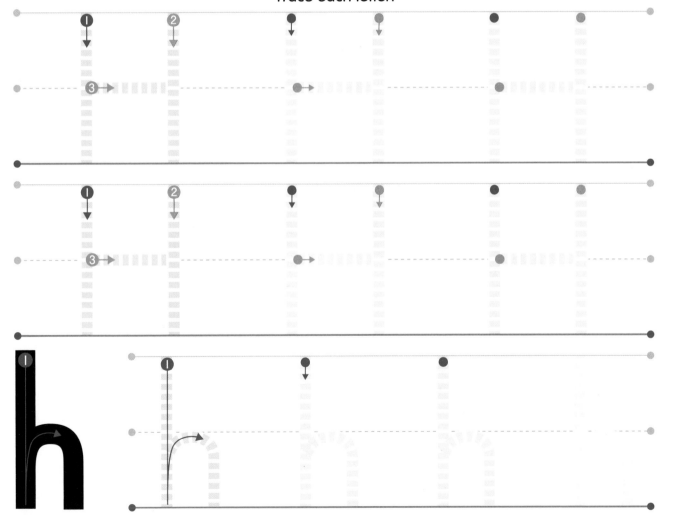

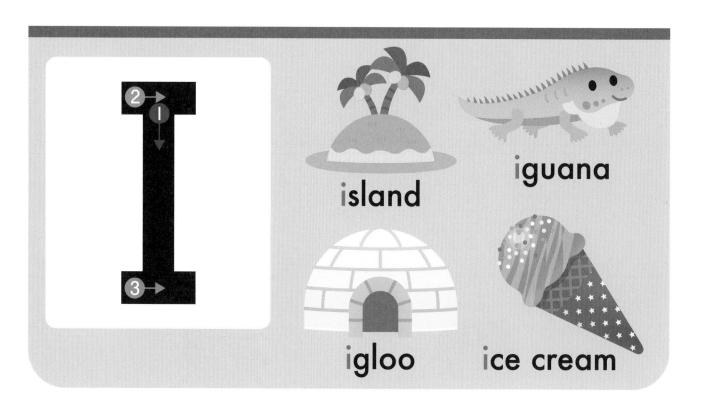

island

iguana

igloo

ice cream

Color the island.

I is for island.

Trace the lines from ➡ to ➡.

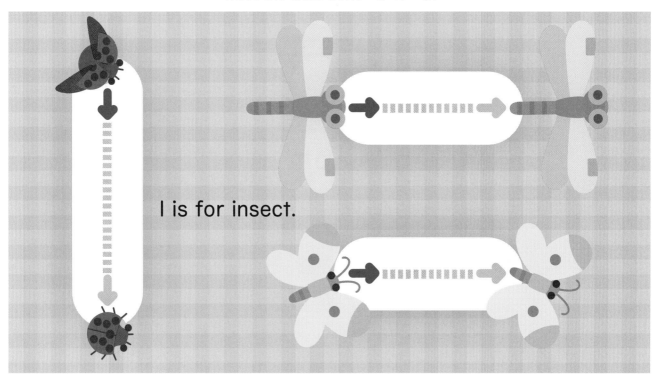

I is for insect.

Trace each letter.

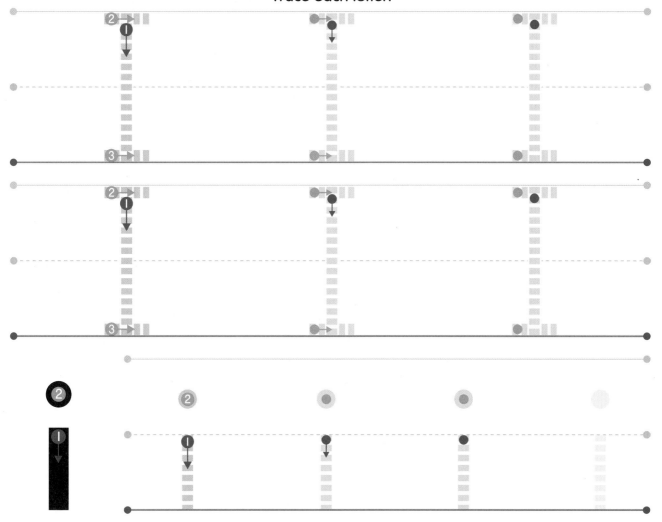

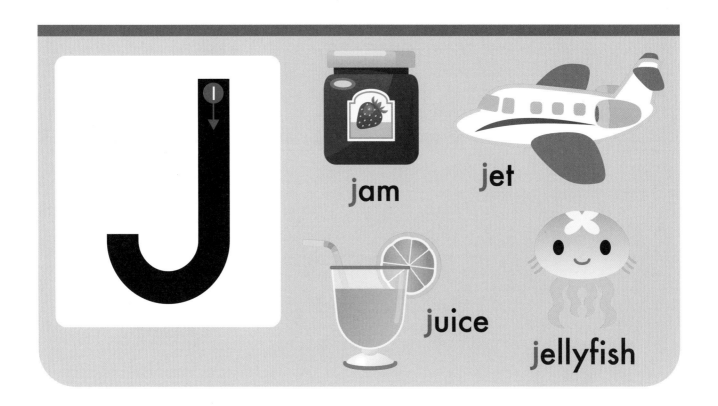

jam

jet

juice

jellyfish

Color the jam.

J is for jam.

Trace the line from ➡ to ➡.

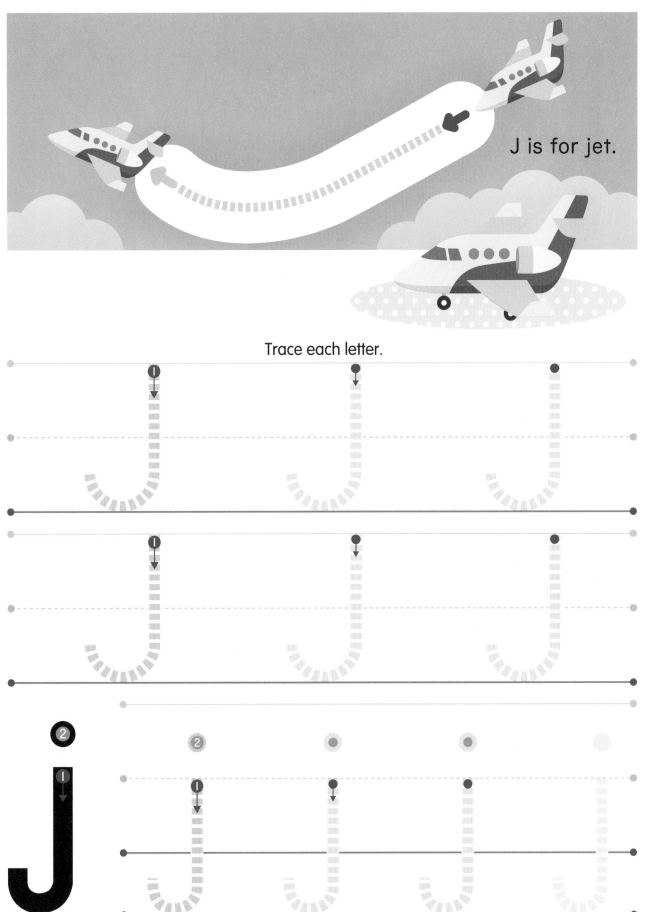

J is for jet.

Trace each letter.

K

koala

key

kiwi

kite

Color the kangaroo.

K is for kangaroo.

Trace the lines from ➡ to ➡.

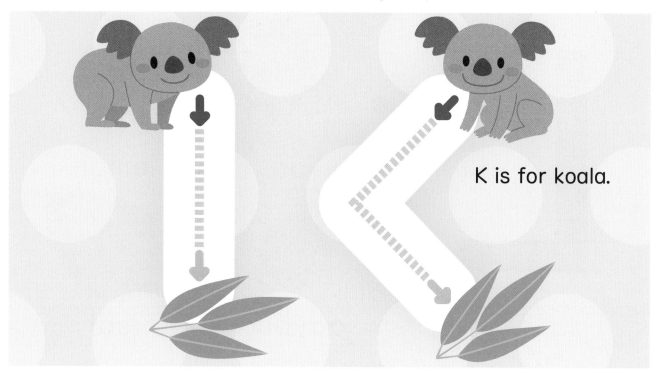

K is for koala.

Trace each letter.

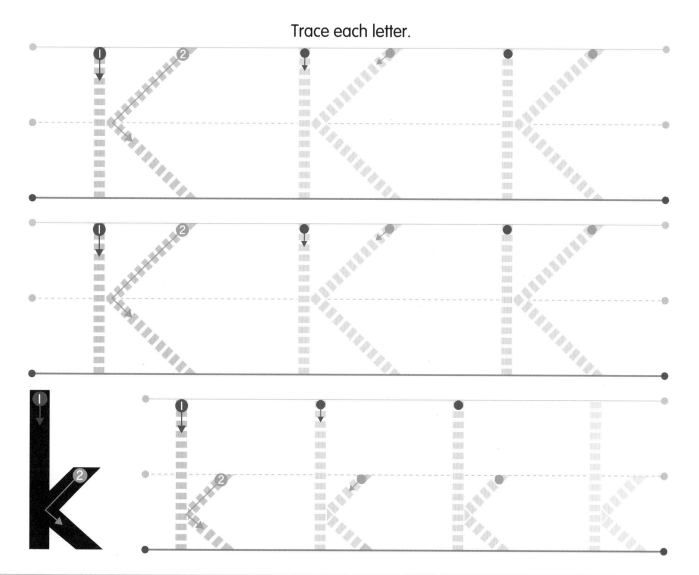

L

lion

lemon

ladybug

leaf

Color the ladybugs.

L is for ladybug.

Trace the lines from ➡ to ➡.

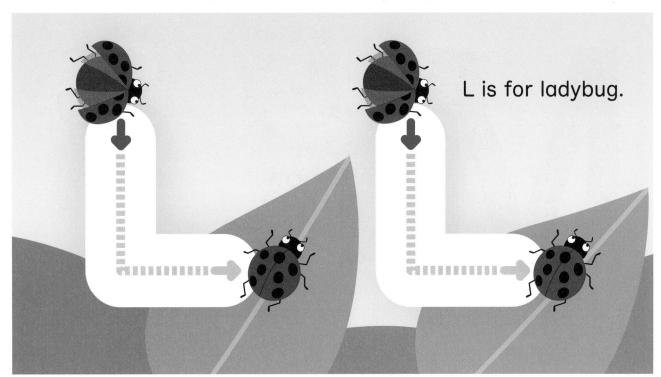

L is for ladybug.

Trace each letter.

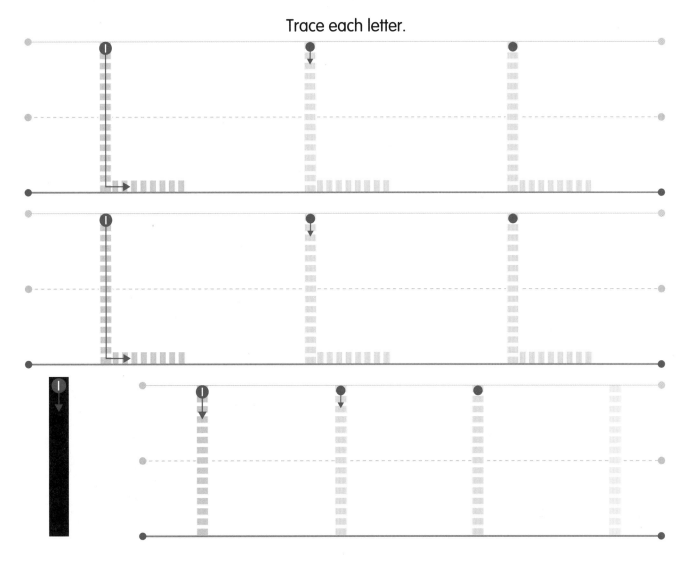

moon

monkey

mouse

milk

MILK

Color the mountain.

M is for mountain.

Trace the lines from ➡ to ➡.

M is for monkey.

Trace each letter.

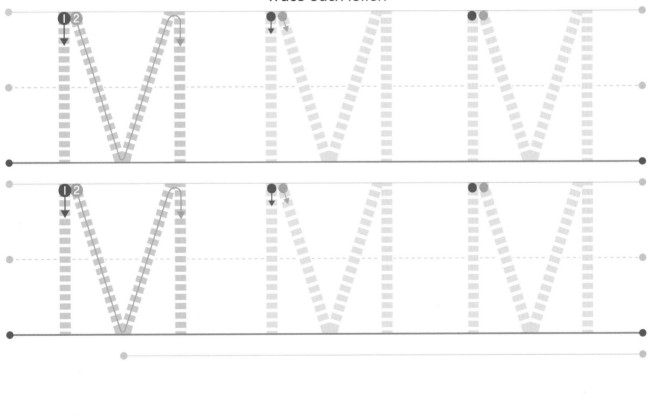

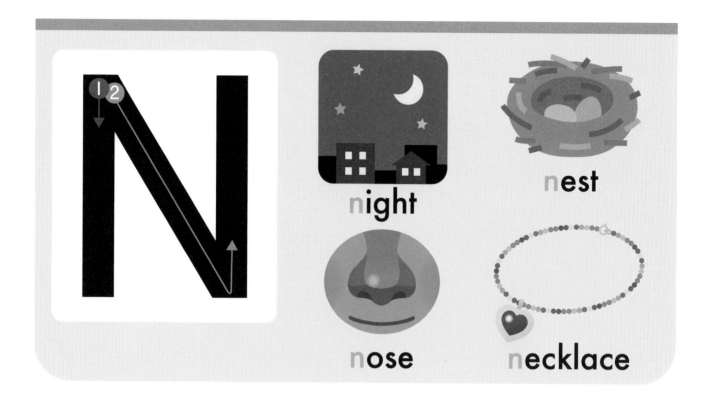

night

nest

nose

necklace

Color the night sky.

N is for night.

Trace the lines from ➡ to ➡.

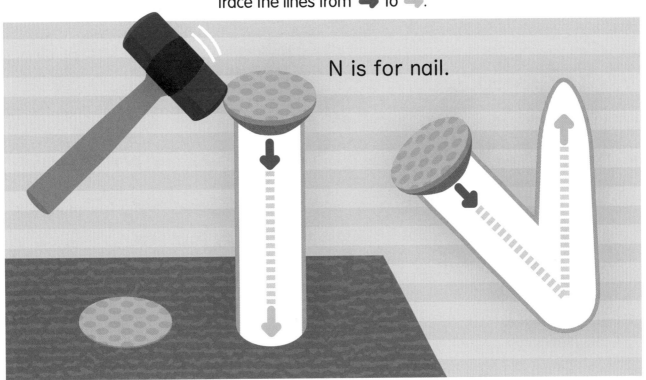

N is for nail.

Trace each letter.

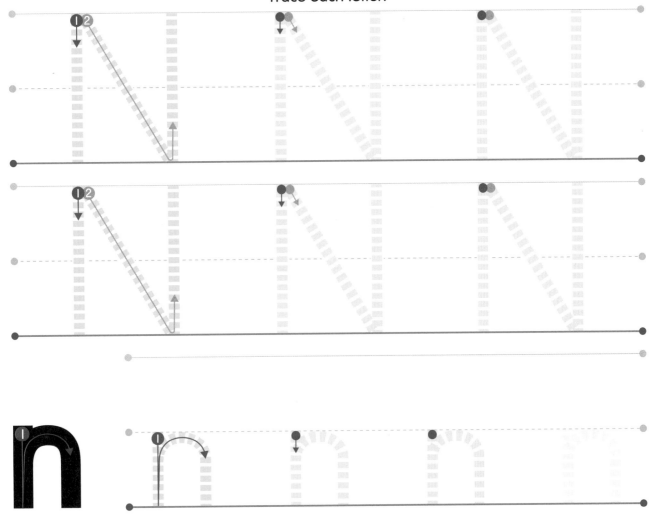

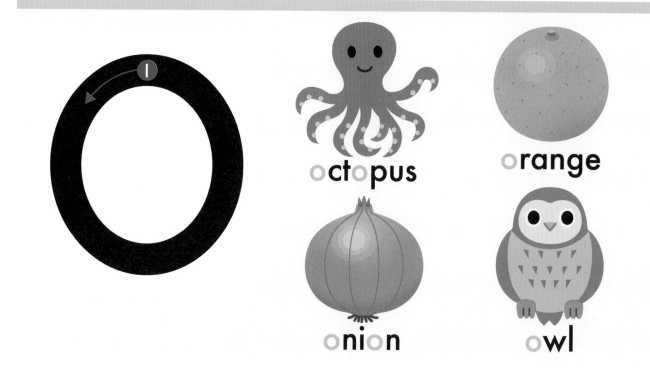

octopus

orange

onion

owl

Color the orange.

O is for orange.

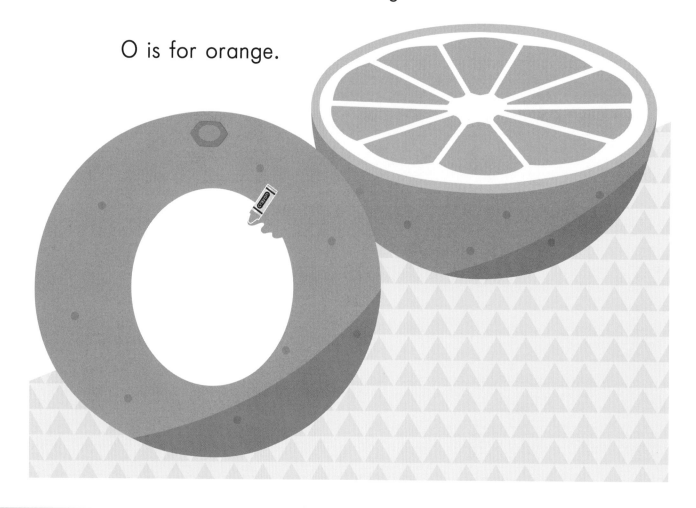

Trace the line from ➡ to ➡.

O is for octopus.

Trace each letter.

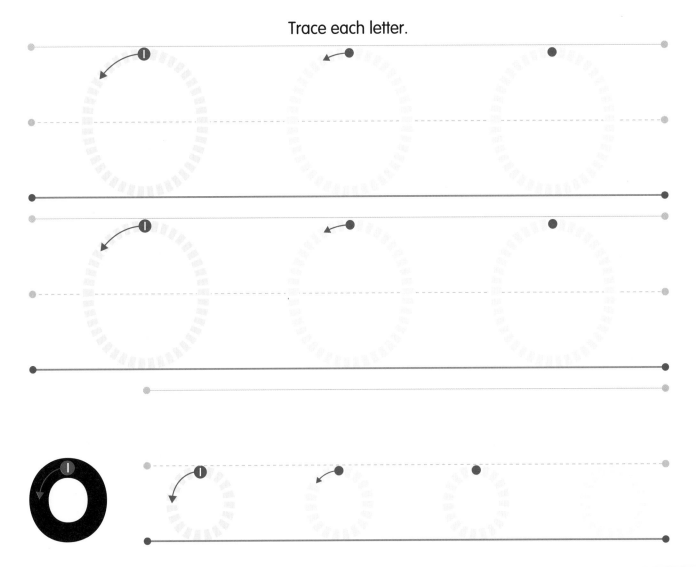

p**anda**

p**ig**

p**ear**

p**enguin**

Color the pineapple.

P is for pineapple.

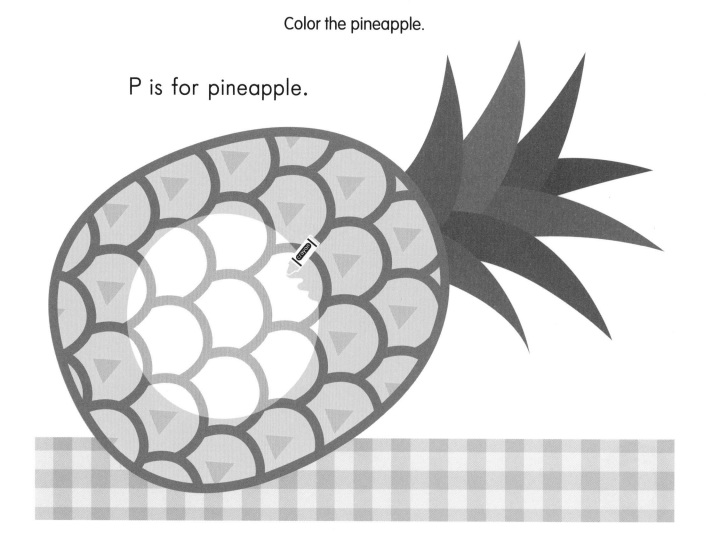

Trace the lines from → to →.

P is for penguin.

Trace each letter.

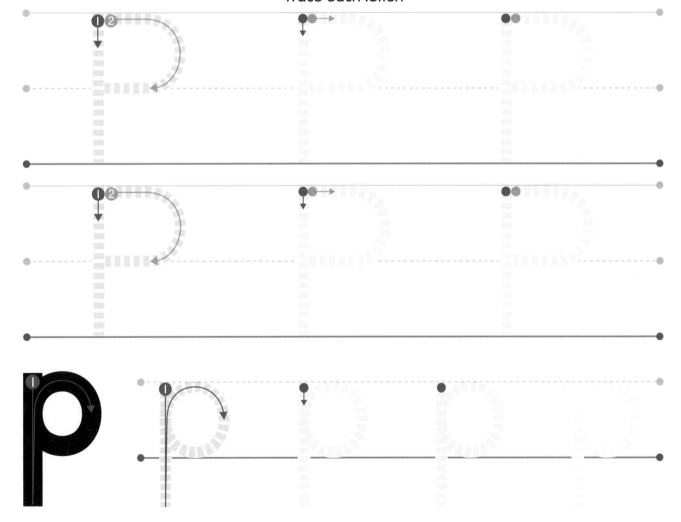

queen

quilt

quail

question

Color the quilt.

Q is for quilt.

Trace the lines from → to →.

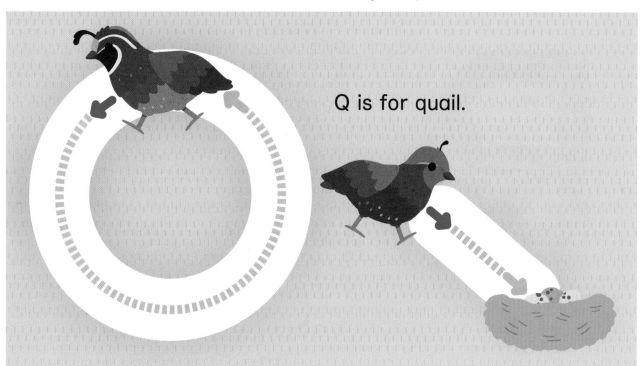

Q is for quail.

Trace each letter.

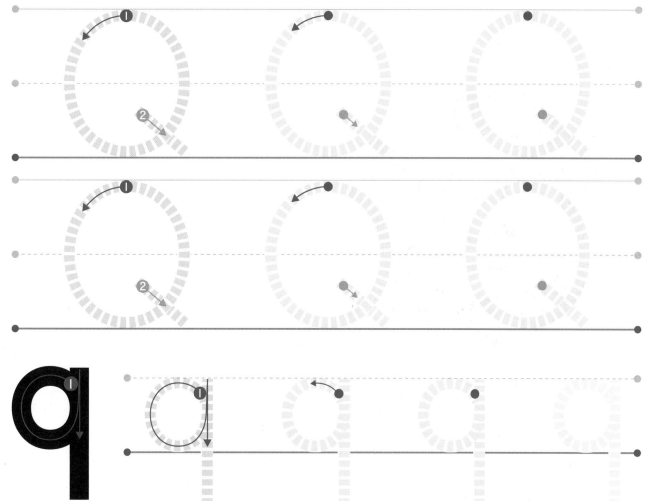

rose

rainbow

rabbit

rocket

Color the roses.

R is for rose.

Trace the lines from ➡ to ➡.

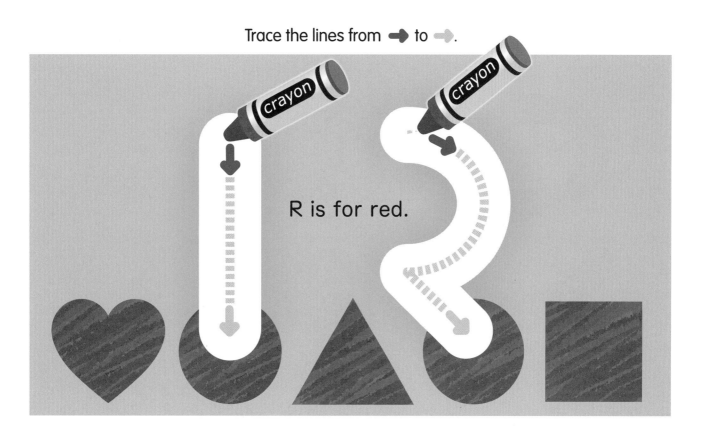

R is for red.

Trace each letter.

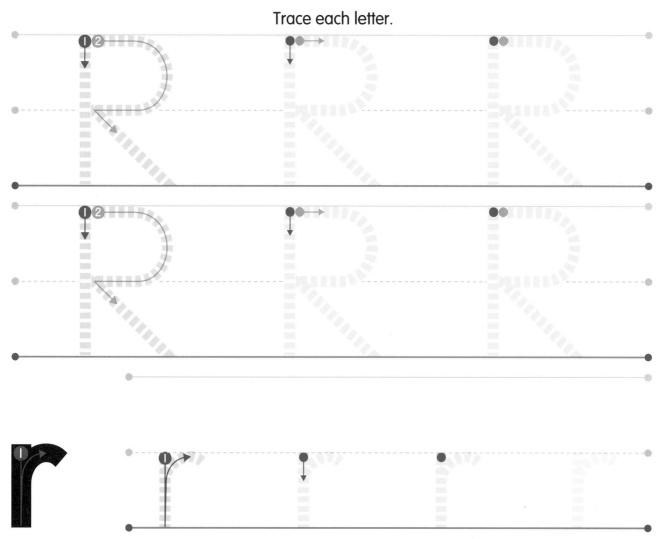

S

star

snake

strawberry

sun

Color the stars.

S is for star.

Trace the lines from → to →.

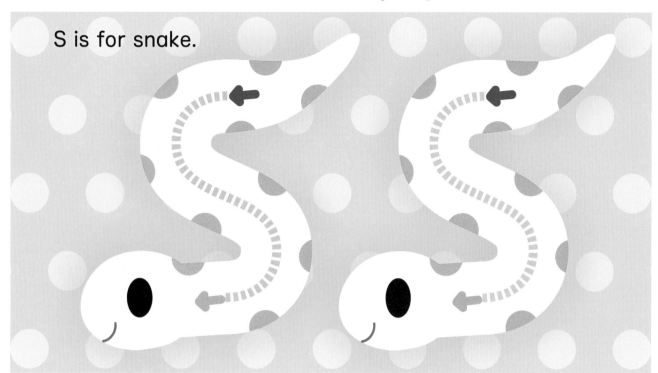

S is for snake.

Trace each letter.

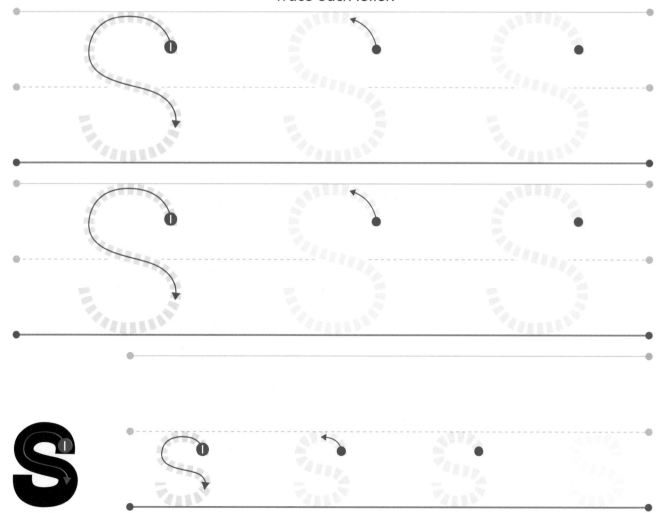

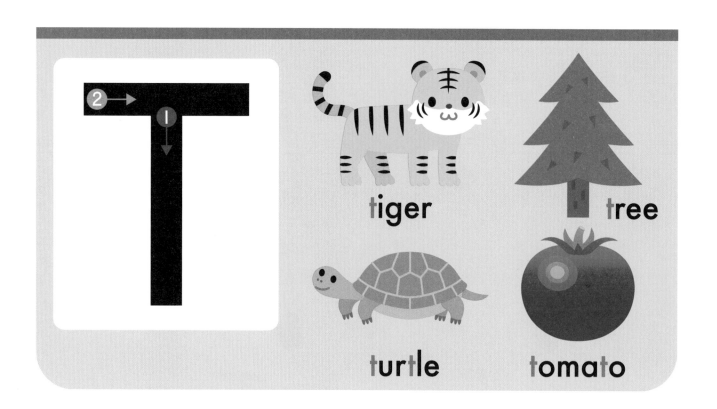

tiger

tree

turtle

tomato

Color the tomato.

T is for tomato.

Trace the lines from → to →.

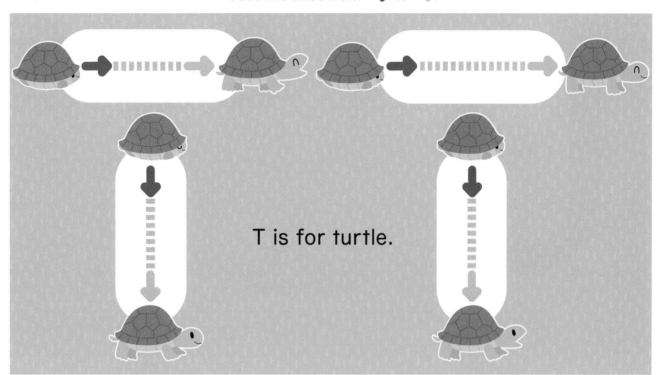

T is for turtle.

Trace each letter.

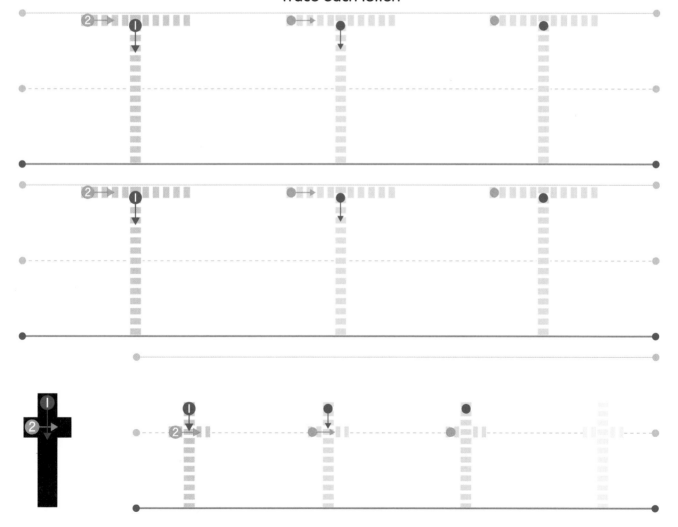

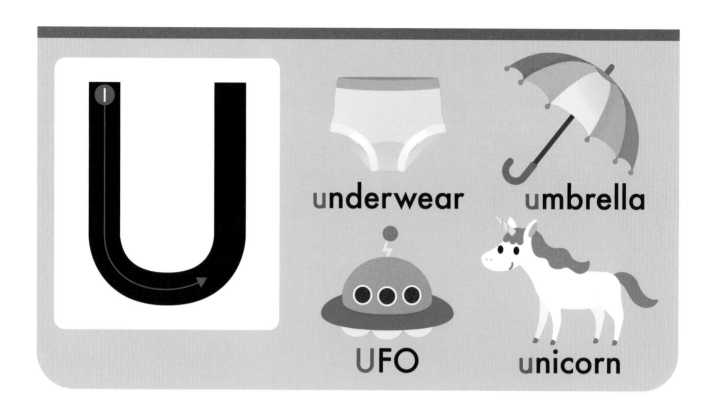

underwear

umbrella

UFO

unicorn

Color the unicorn.

U is for unicorn.

Trace the lines from ➡ to ➡.

U is for unicorn.

Trace each letter.

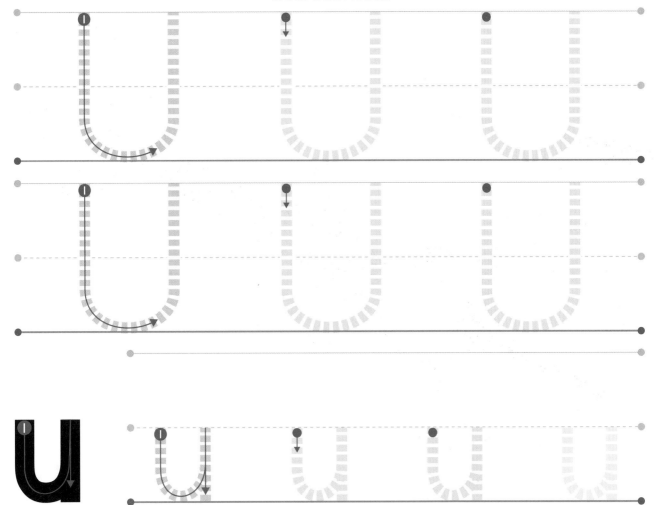

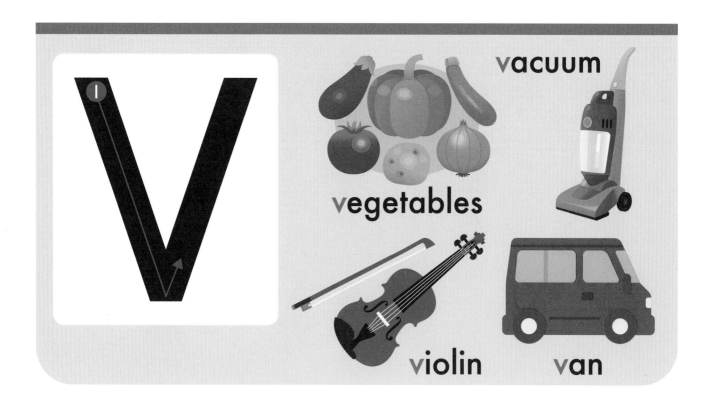

vacuum

vegetables

violin

van

Color the violin.

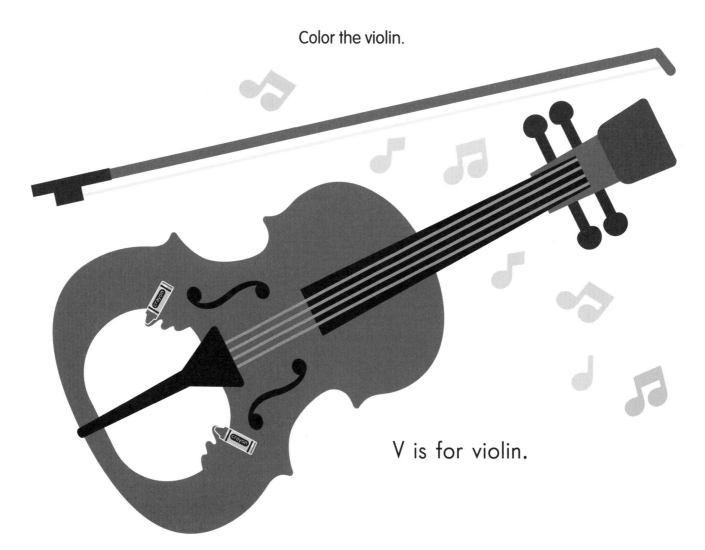

V is for violin.

Trace the lines from ➡ to ➡.

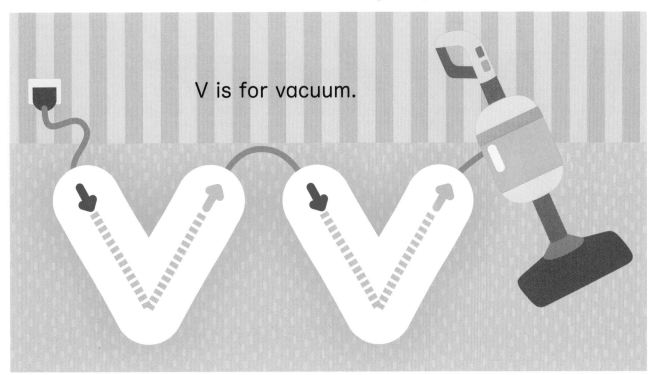

V is for vacuum.

Trace each letter.

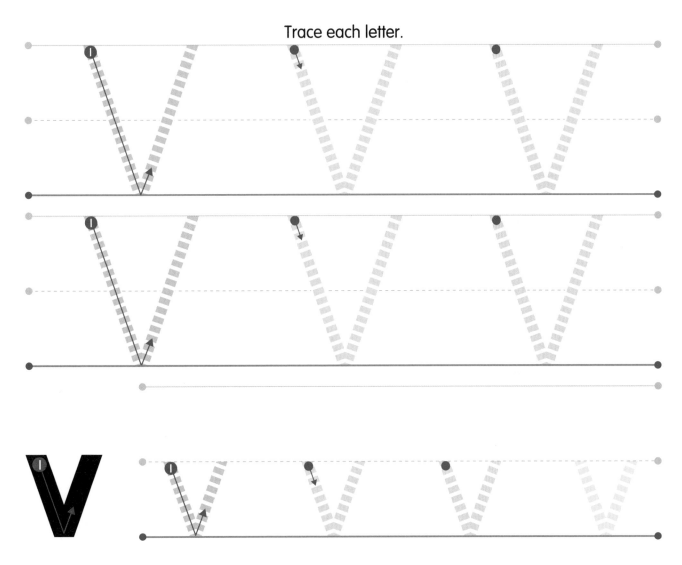

W

whale

window

watermelon

wolf

Color the whale.

W is for whale.

Trace the line from ➡ to ➡.

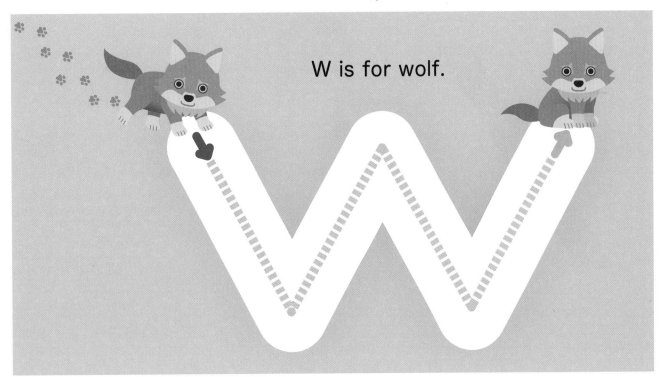

W is for wolf.

Trace each letter.

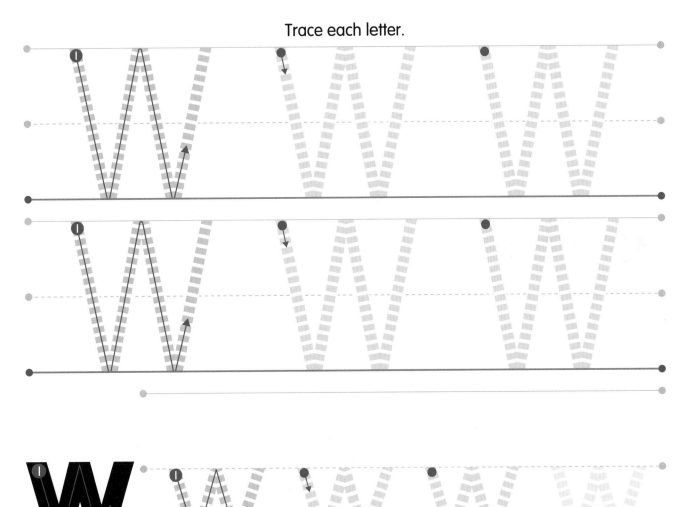

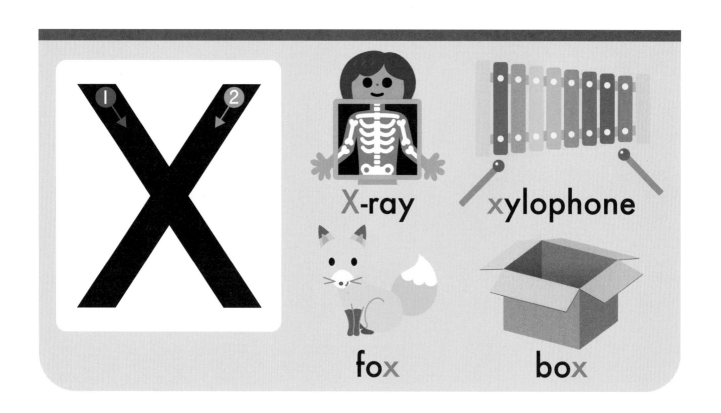

X-ray

xylophone

fox

box

Color the fox.

X is for fox.

Trace the lines from ➡ to ➡.

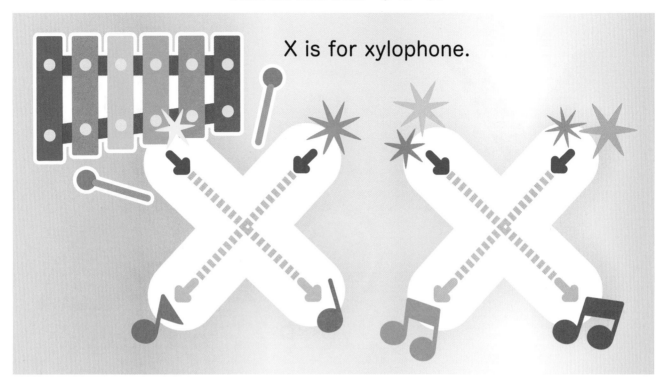

X is for xylophone.

Trace each letter.

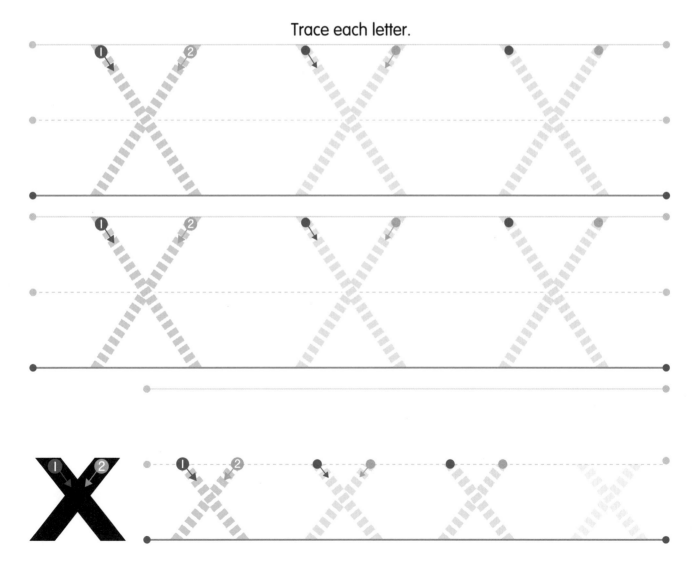

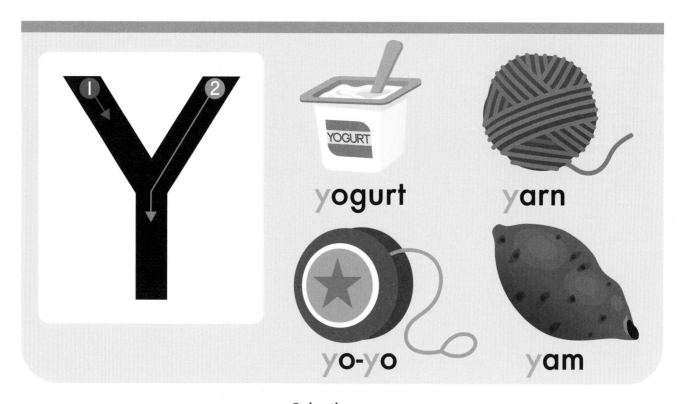

yogurt   **y**arn

yo-yo   **y**am

Color the yarn.

Y is for yarn.

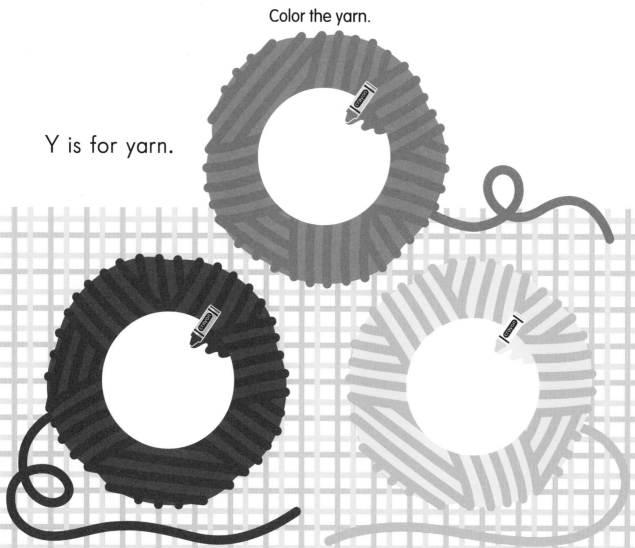

Trace the lines from ➡ to ➡.

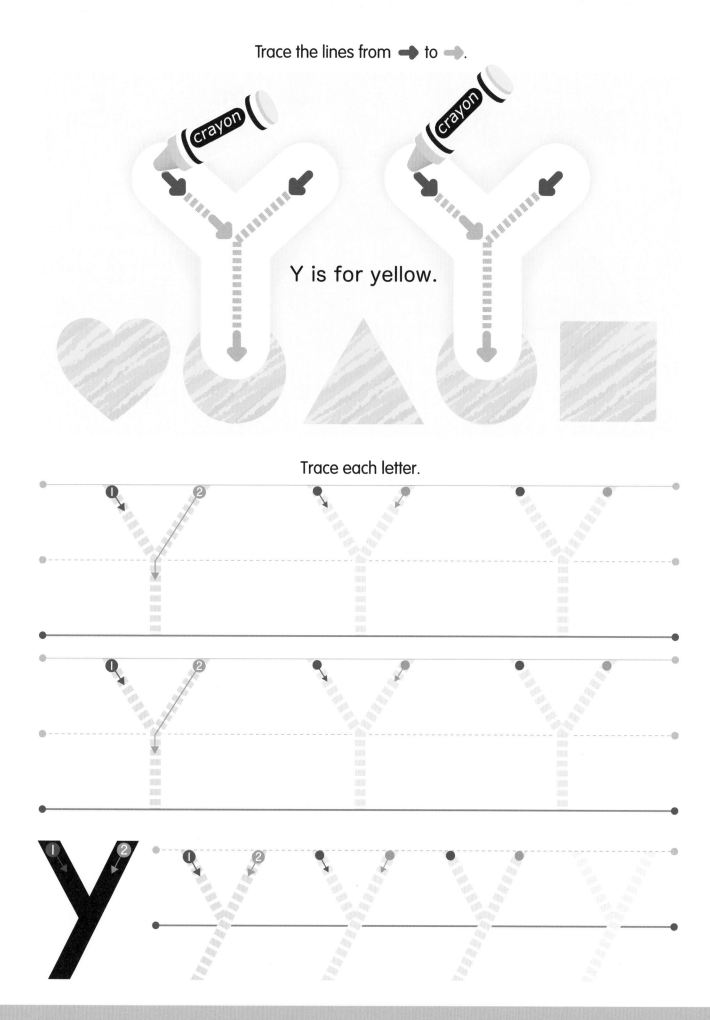

Y is for yellow.

Trace each letter.

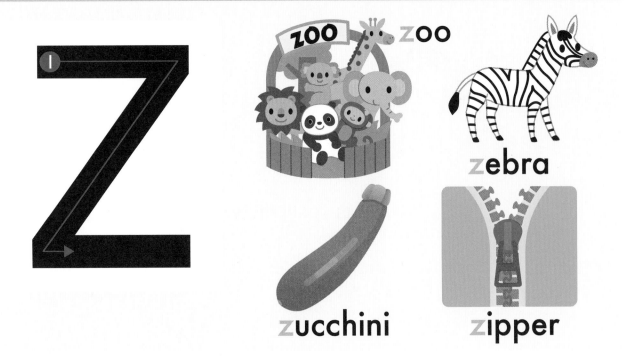

zoo zoo

zebra

zucchini

zipper

Trace the lines from ➡ to ➡.

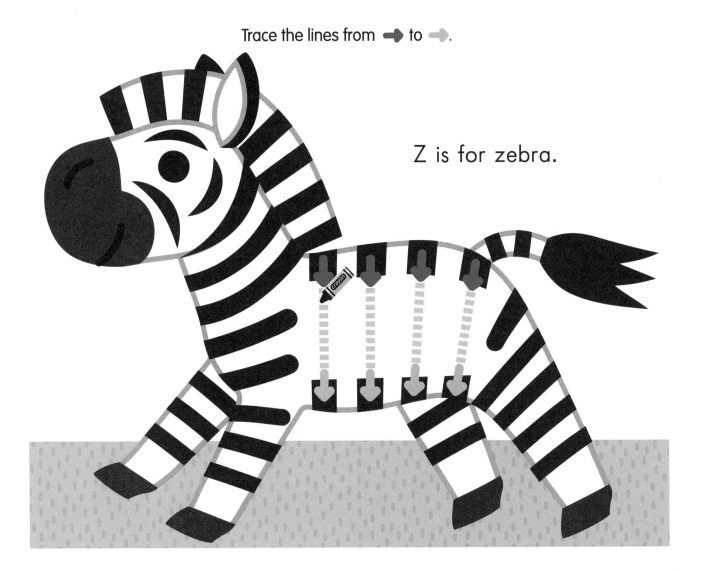

Z is for zebra.

Trace the lines from ➡ to ➡.

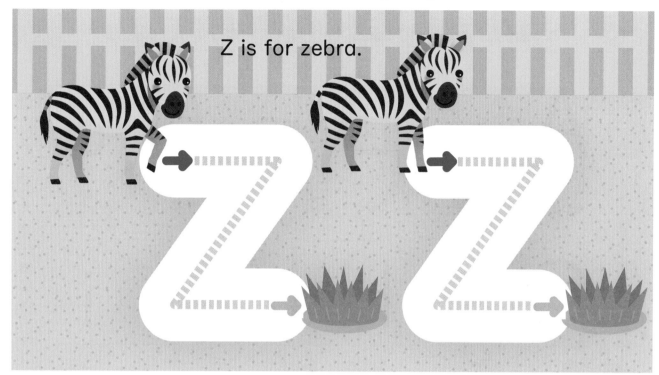

Z is for zebra.

Trace each letter.

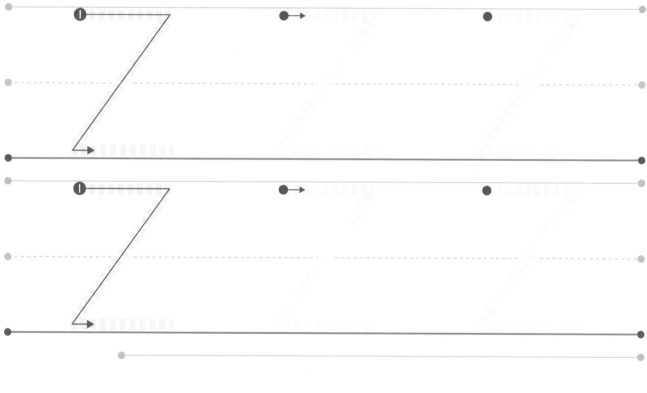

ALPHABET

A a apple

B b bee

C c cat

G g gorilla

H h hat

I i ice cream

M m monkey

N n necklace

O o octopus

S s strawberry

T t train

U u umbrella

Y y yo-yo

Z z zebra

D d
dog

E e
elephant

F f
fish

J j
jet

K k
king

L l
lamb

P p
penguin

Q q
queen

R r
rabbit

V v
violin

W w
whale

X x
xylophone

Alphabet Maze

Draw a line from ➡ to ➡, following the path from A→B→C→D→E.
Say the name of the object and letter as you pass through them.

Match Uppercase and Lowercase Letters

Draw a line to match each uppercase letter to its lowercase letter.
If difficult, draw a line matching each object and its shadow.

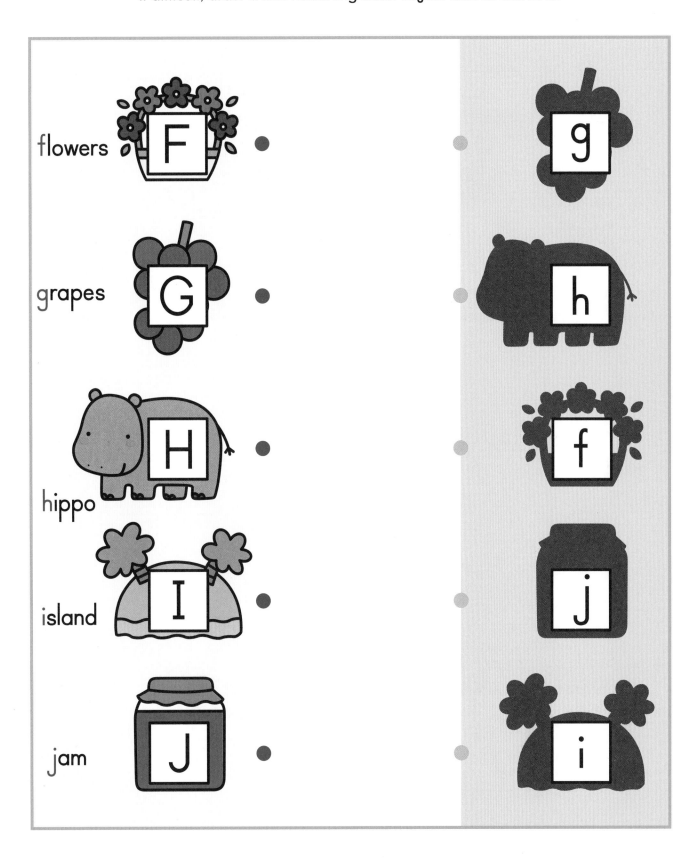

flowers

grapes

hippo

island

jam

Match Uppercase and Lowercase Letters

Draw a line from ➡ to ➡ to match uppercase and lowercase letters.

Alphabet Maze

Draw a line from ➡ to ➡, following the path from P→Q→R→S→T→U.
Say the name of the object and letter as you pass through them.

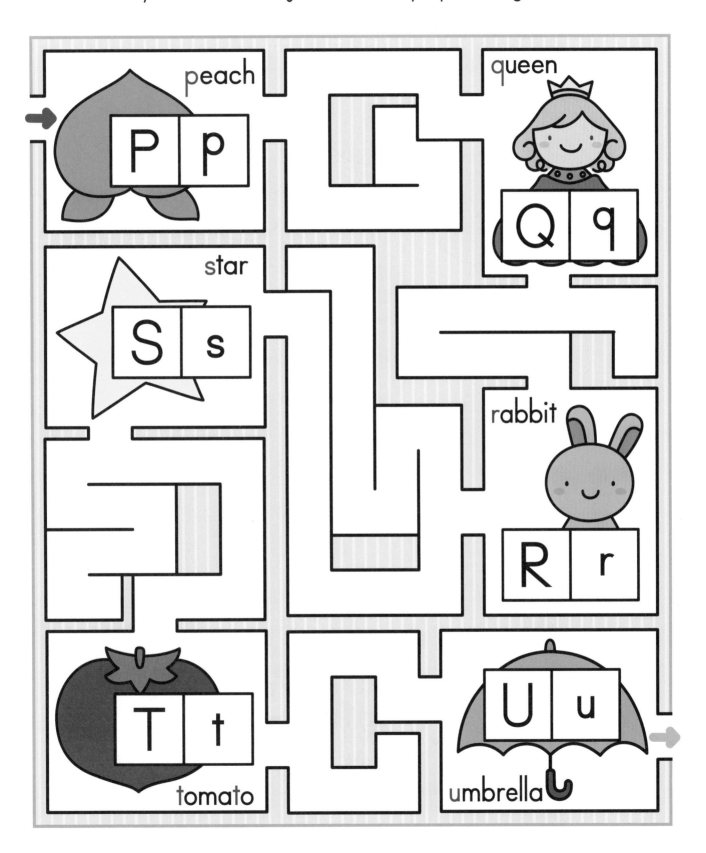

peach

P p

queen

Q q

star

S s

rabbit

R r

tomato

T t

umbrella

U u

Match Uppercase and Lowercase Letters

Draw a line from ➡ to ➡ to match uppercase and lowercase letters.

Connect the Dots

Connect the dots in order of the alphabet.

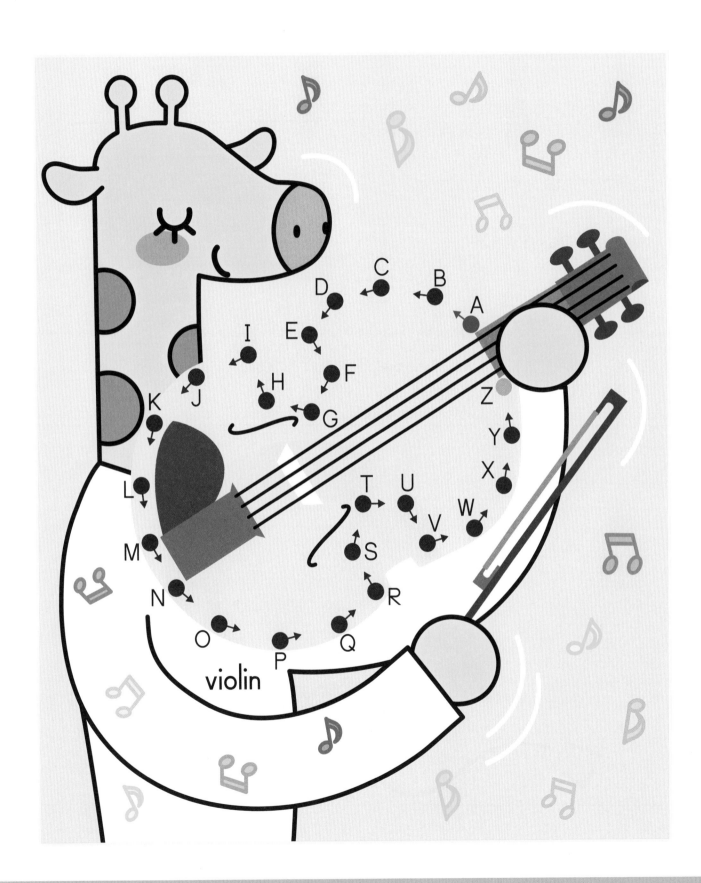

violin

one

Count the object and say "one."

Color the balloon. Count it: "One."

1 balloon

Find I ship and circle it. Then, find the number I.

example

Trace the numbers.

2

two

Count the objects and say "two."

Color the excavators. Count them: "One, two."

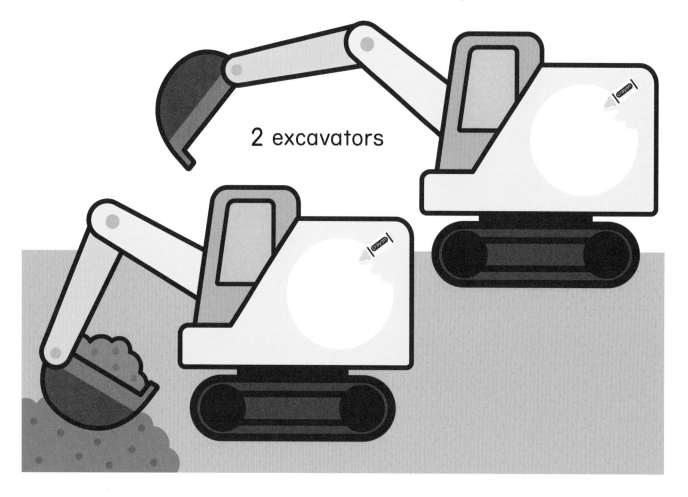

2 excavators

Find 2 bears and circle them. Then, find the number 2.

Trace the numbers.

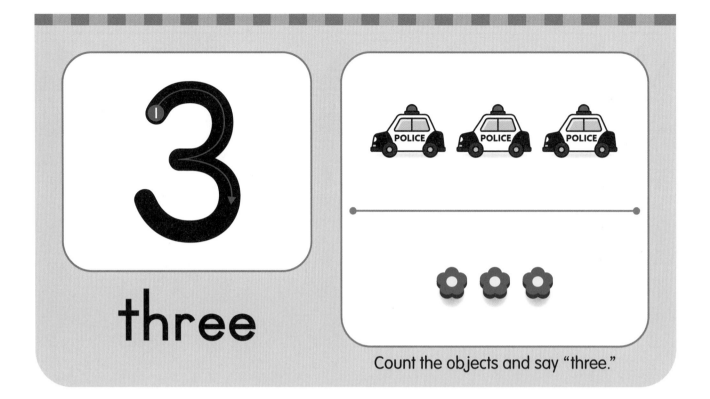

3

three

Count the objects and say "three."

Color the carrots. Count them: "One, two, three."

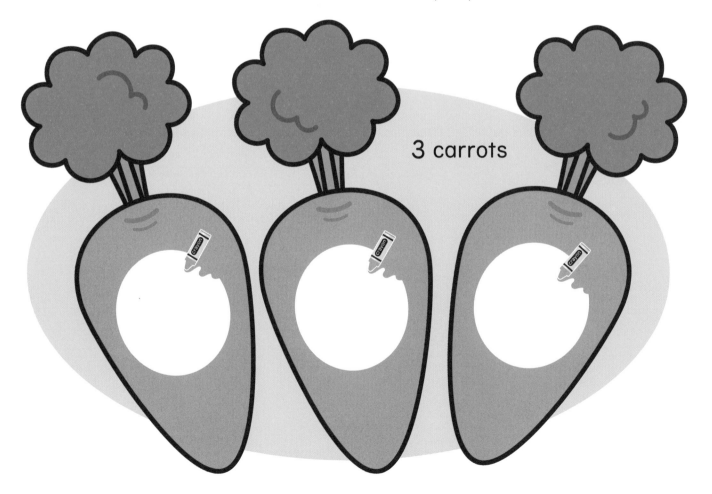

3 carrots

Find 3 excavators and circle them. Then, find the number 3.

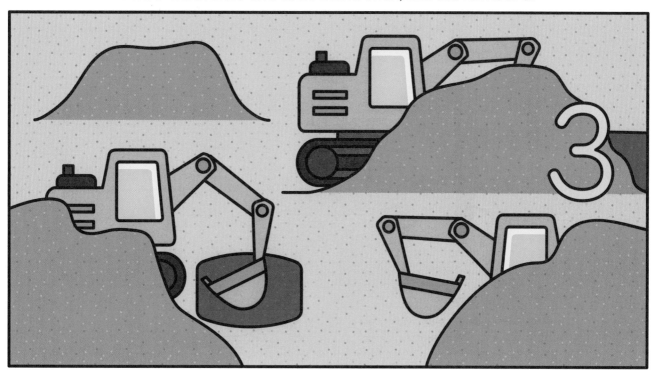

Trace the numbers.

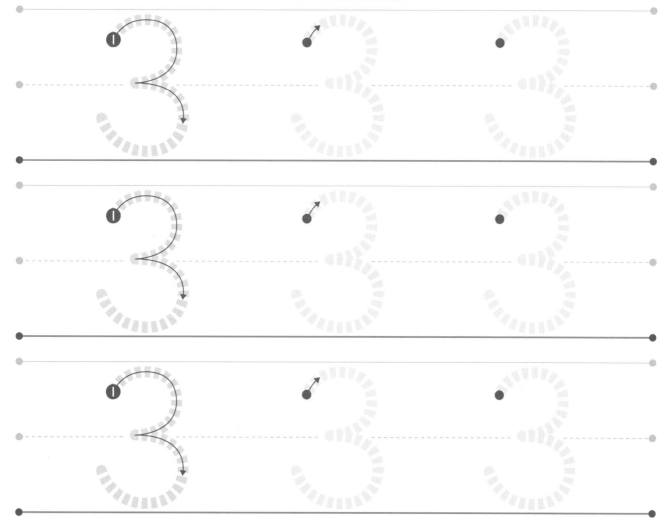

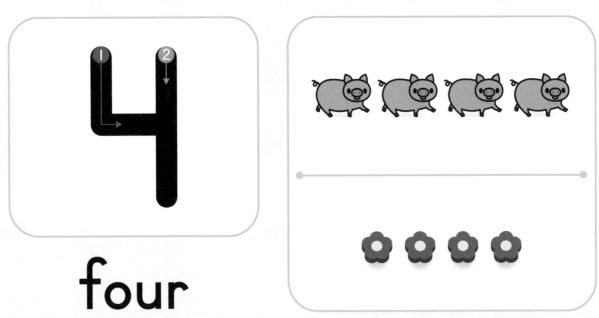

four

Count the objects and say "four."

Color the stars. Count them: "One, two, three, four."

4 stars

Find 4 penguins and circle them. Then, find the number 4.

Trace the numbers.

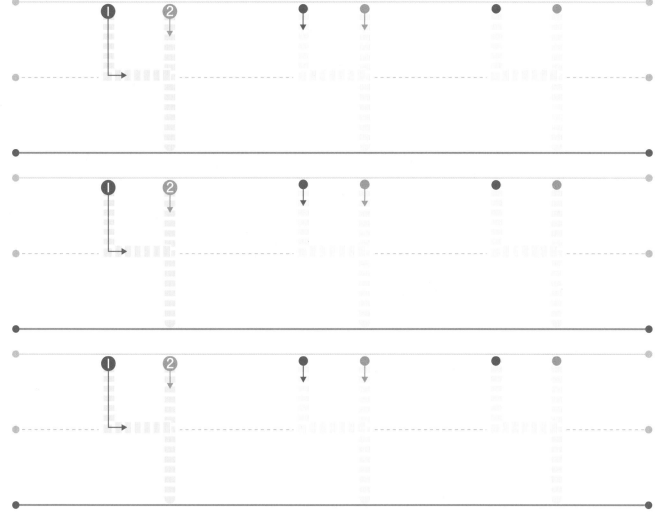

5

five

Count the objects and say "five."

Color the fish. Count them: "One, two, three, four, five."

5 fish

Find 5 hedgehogs and circle them. Then, find the number 5.

Trace the numbers.

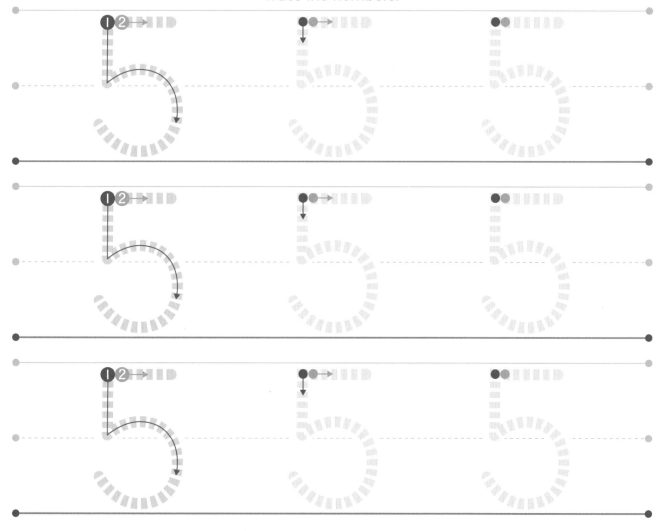

6

six

Count the objects and say "six."

Color the trees. Count them: "One, two, three, four, five, six."

Find 6 koalas and circle them. Then, find the number 6.

Trace the numbers.

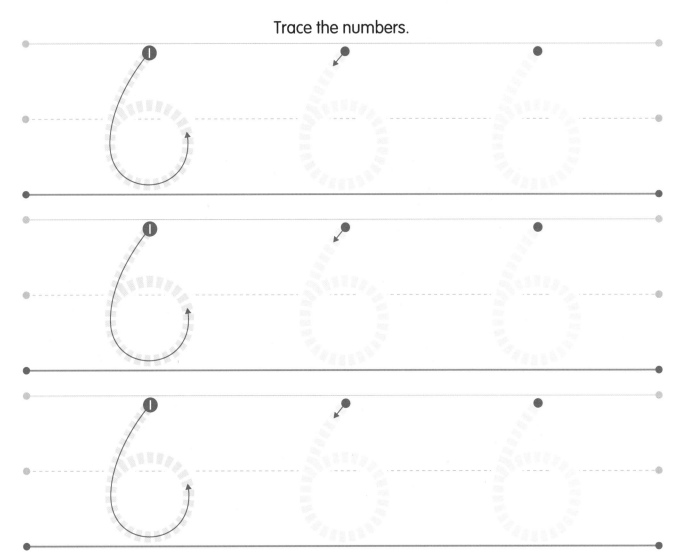

seven

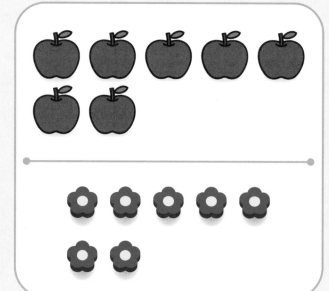

Count the objects and say "seven."

Color the crabs. Count them: "One, two, three, four, five, six, seven."

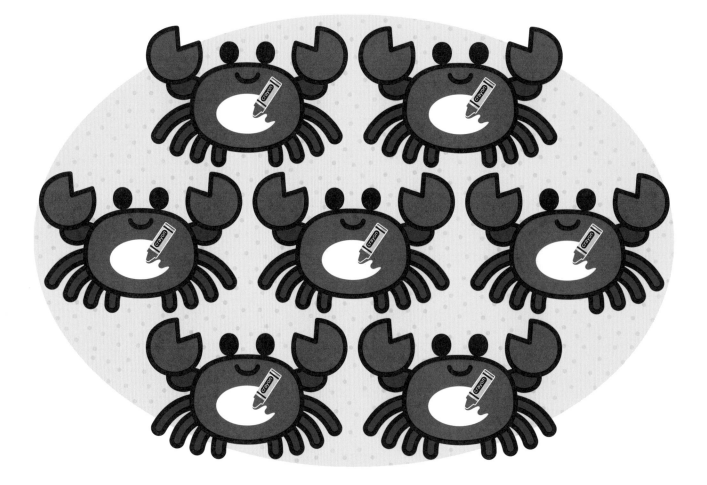

Find 7 pumpkins and circle them. Then, find the number 7.

Trace the numbers.

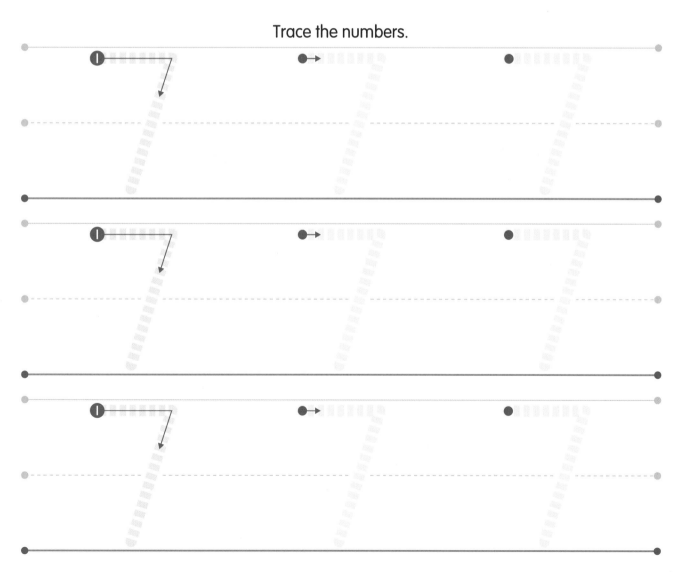

8

eight

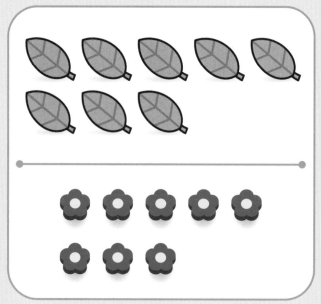

Count the objects and say "eight."

Color the flowers. Count them: "One, two, three, four, five, six, seven, eight."

Find 8 lizards and circle them. Then, find the number 8.

Trace the numbers.

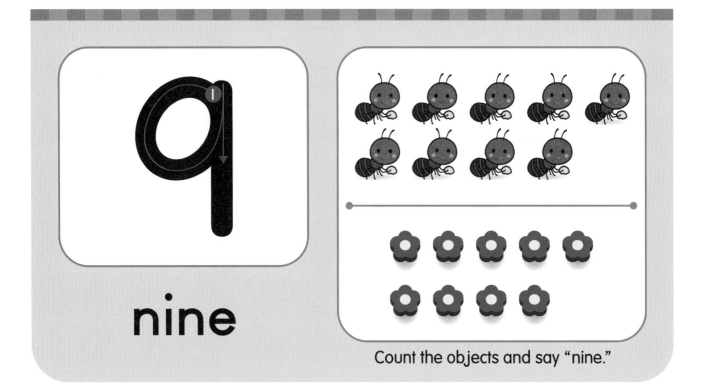

nine

Count the objects and say "nine."

Color the candies. Count them: "One, two, three, four, five, six, seven, eight, nine."

Find 9 bees and circle them. Then, find the number 9.

Trace the numbers.

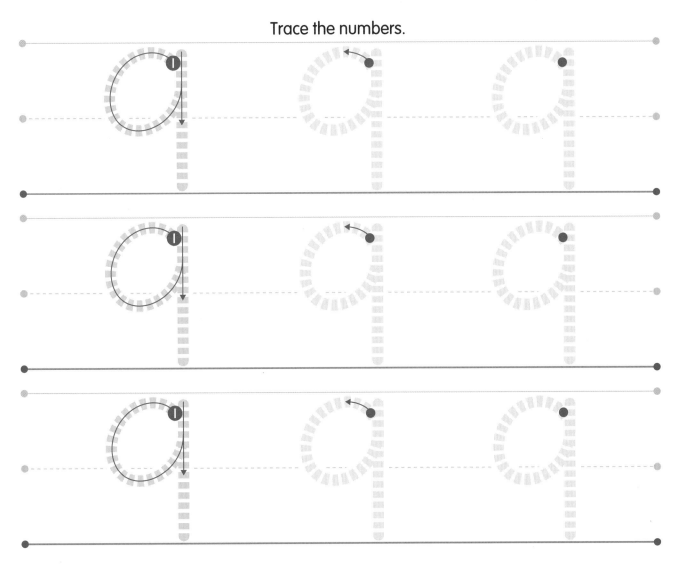

Count the objects and say "ten."

Color the jellyfish. Count them: "One, two, three, four, five, six, seven, eight, nine, ten."

Find 10 lollipops and circle them. Then, find the number 10.

Trace the numbers.

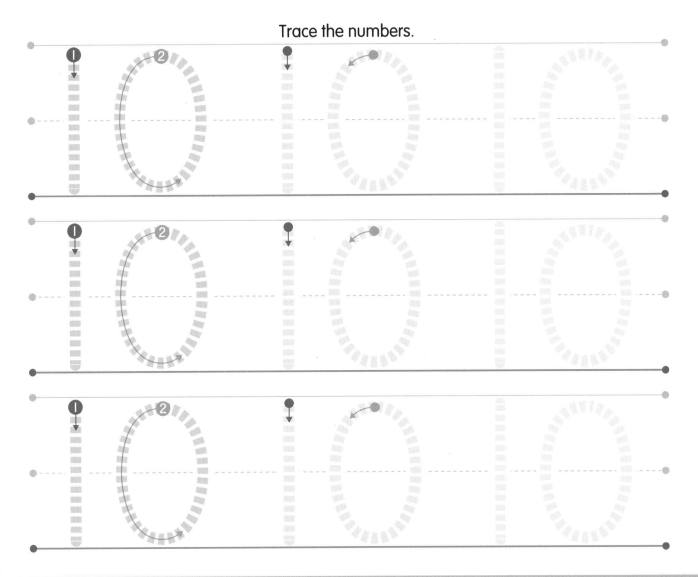

Count 1 to 10

1		
2		
3		
4		
5		
6		
7		
8		
9		
10		

Color by Number

Color the number 1 using any color you like.
What do you see?

Color by Number

Color the number 2 using any color you like.
What do you see?

NUMBERS

Color by Number

Color the number 3 in **RED** and the number 4 in **BROWN**.
What do you see?

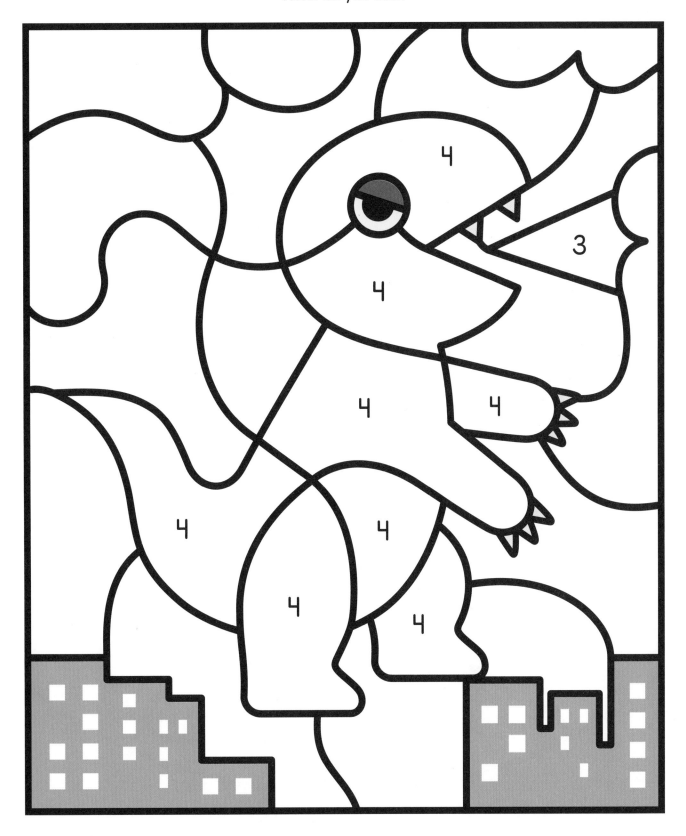

Color by Number

Color the number 5 in YELLOW, the number 6 in GREEN, and the number 7 in RED.
What do you see?

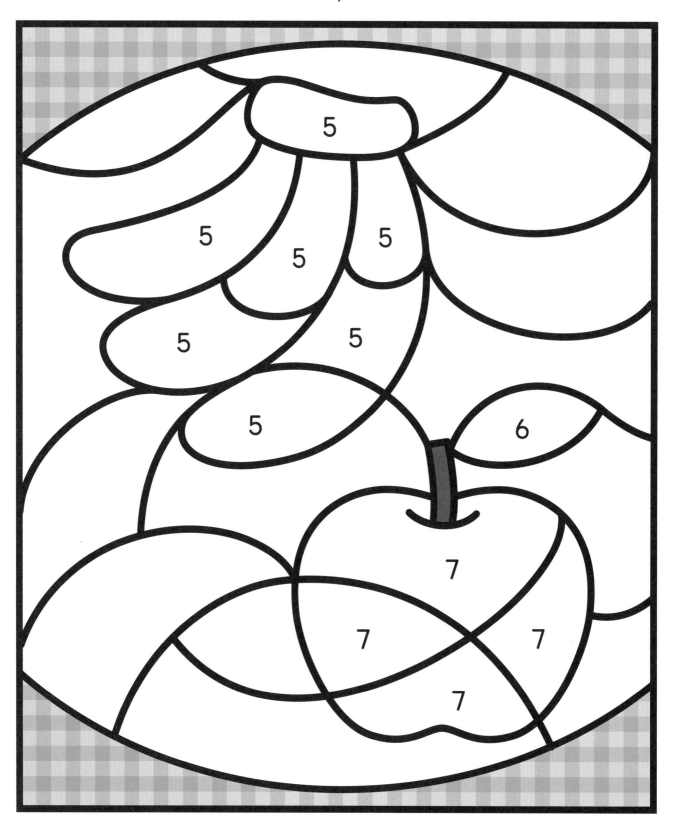

Color by Number

Color the number 8 in YELLOW, the number 9 in ORANGE, and the number 10 in BLUE.
What do you see?

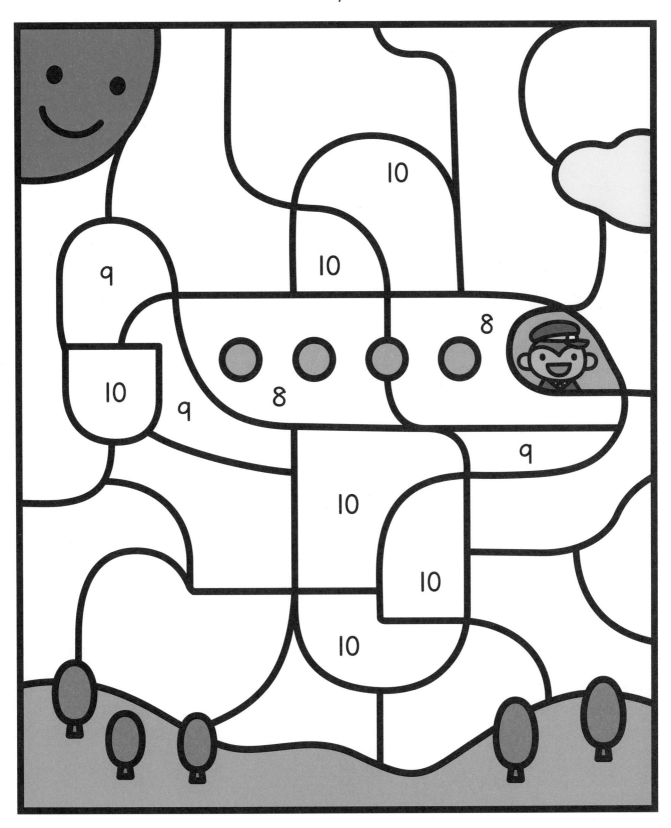

Sailors and Swimmers

Find and trace the triangles. Then, color them using any colors you like.

Circles in the Sky

Trace the circles. Then, color them using any colors you like.

Kite-Flying Fun!

Trace the ▬▬▬ lines to create rectangles. Then, color them using any colors you like.

COLORS & SHAPES

Lily Pads on the Pond

Find all the circles in the picture. Color them GREEN. Can the little frogs hop from one lily pad to another to get to their home on the other side of the pond?

Build a Robot

Find the rectangles and squares and color them BLUE.

COLORS & SHAPES

Apple Picking Time!

Trace the ◯. Then, color each circle **RED**.
When you're done, draw more apples on the tree.

Help Everyone Stay Dry!

It's raining. Trace the △. Then, draw triangles to give each animal an umbrella.

COLORS & SHAPES

Special Delivery

Trace the ☐ to draw more packages on the truck. Color them using any colors you like. When you're done, draw some more packages.

Have a Grape Day!

Trace the ◯ **PURPLE**.
Then, draw and color more circles to make more grapes.

Finish the Fishies

Trace the △ and the ▬▬▬ lines. Then, draw lines to finish the triangles, making 3 fish. Circle the smallest fish.

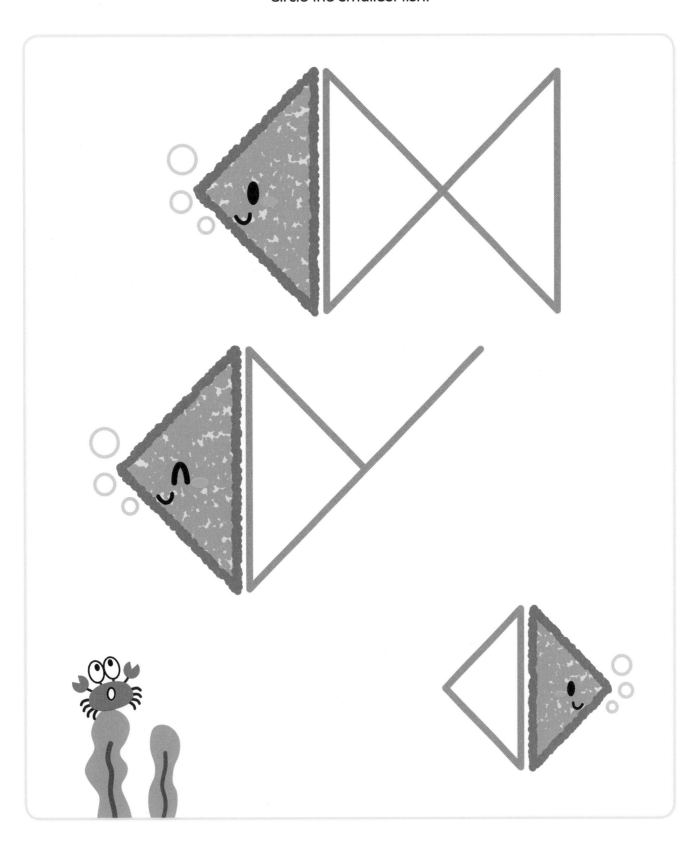

More Ice Cream

Look at the scoops of ice cream below. Notice how each ◯ is smaller than the one beneath it.
Draw ◯ to make more scoops of ice cream. Color the ◯ using any colors you like.

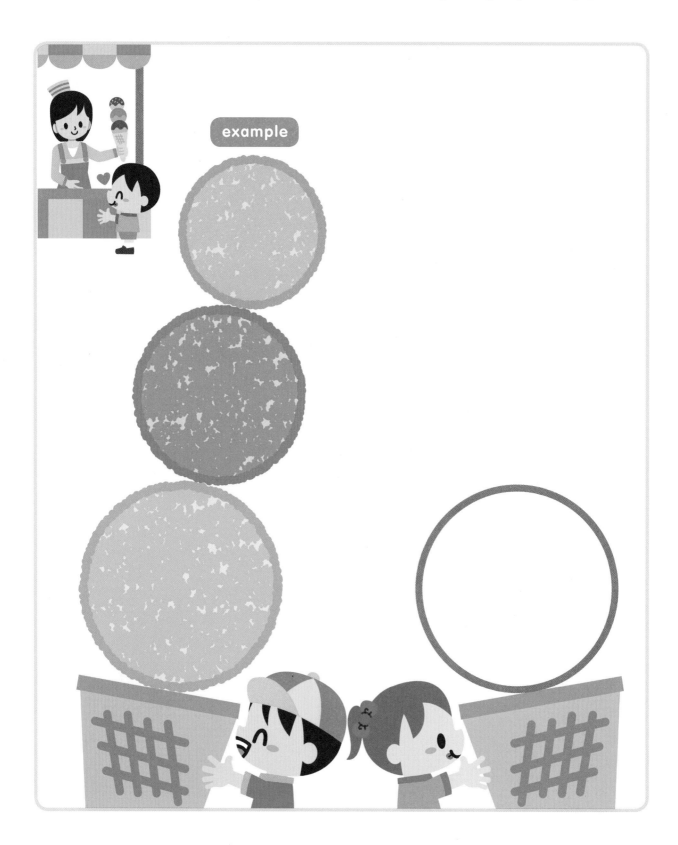

example

Feeling Fruity?

Trace and draw the fruit below to match the picture in the example box. Color them with the matching colors. When you are done, say "watermelon," "cherries," and "orange."

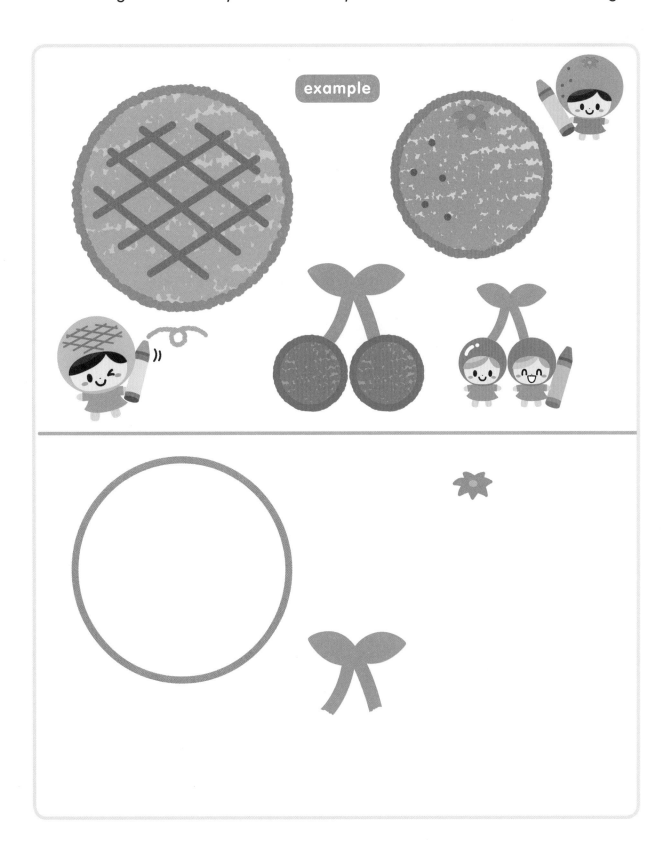

Tweet, Tweet

Trace the ━━━━━ lines and shapes. Then, draw lines to finish the bird on the bottom.
Look at the example if you need help. Color the bird using any colors you like.

example

COLORS & SHAPES

Learn to Draw Bows

Look at the example box. Then, practice drawing bows in the girl's hair and on the girl's hat. Add bows to her shirt, too!

Hungry, Hungry Dinos

Look at the example box below. Then, practice drawing grass on the ground. Make sure to put some in front of the blue dinosaur. It's hungry!

Finish the Triangles

Trace the △ and the ▬▬▬ lines. Then, draw lines to finish each triangle so each picture on the right matches the example picture on the left.

example

example

example

Spot the Shapes

Color the shapes below so the pictures on the right match the example pictures.

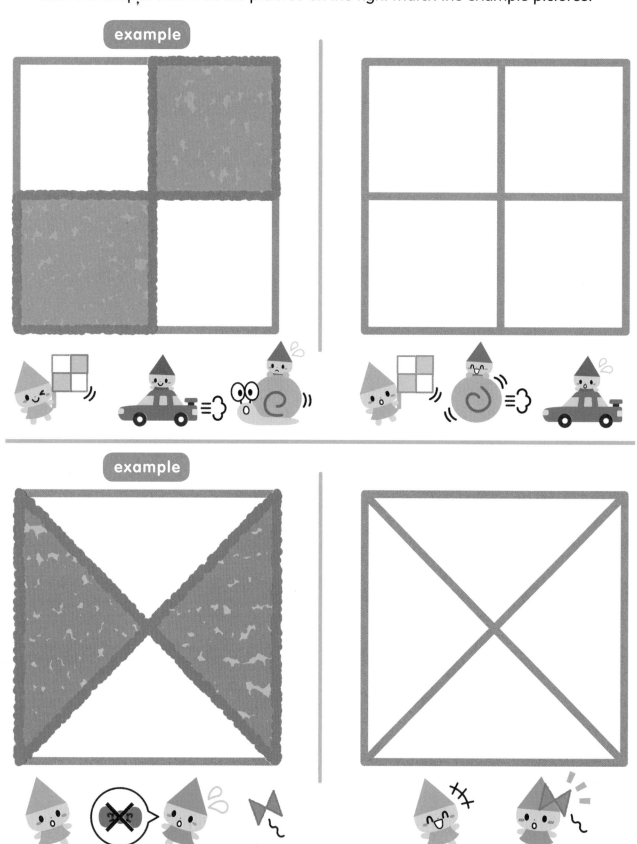

Copy That!

Color the shapes below so the pictures on the right match the example pictures.

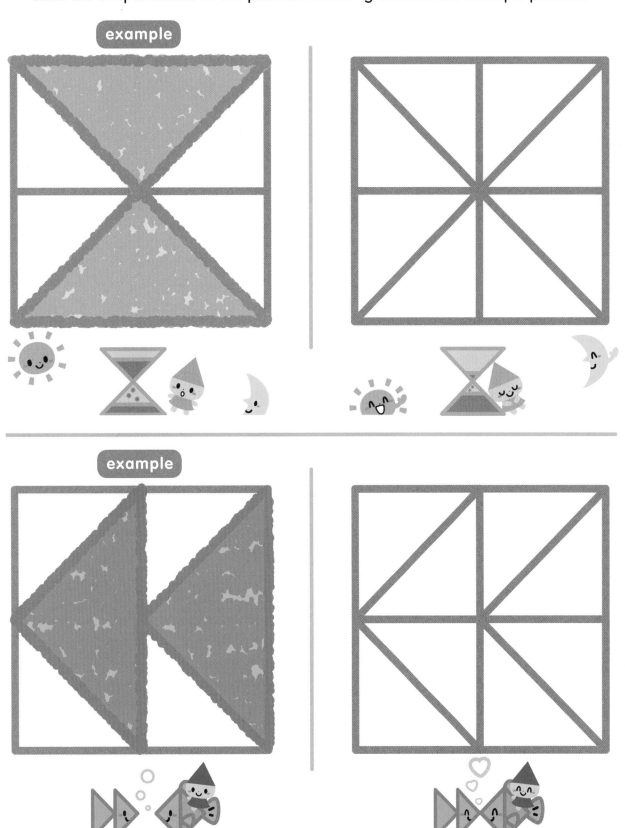

example

example

Foxes and Pinwheels

Color the shapes below so the pictures on the right match the example pictures.

example

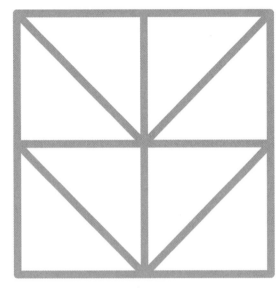

example

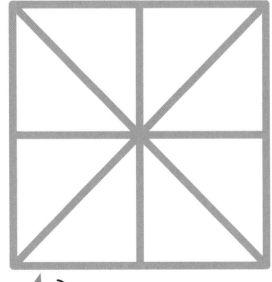

Design a T-Shirt

Decorate the T-shirt using any colors, patterns, or pictures you like.

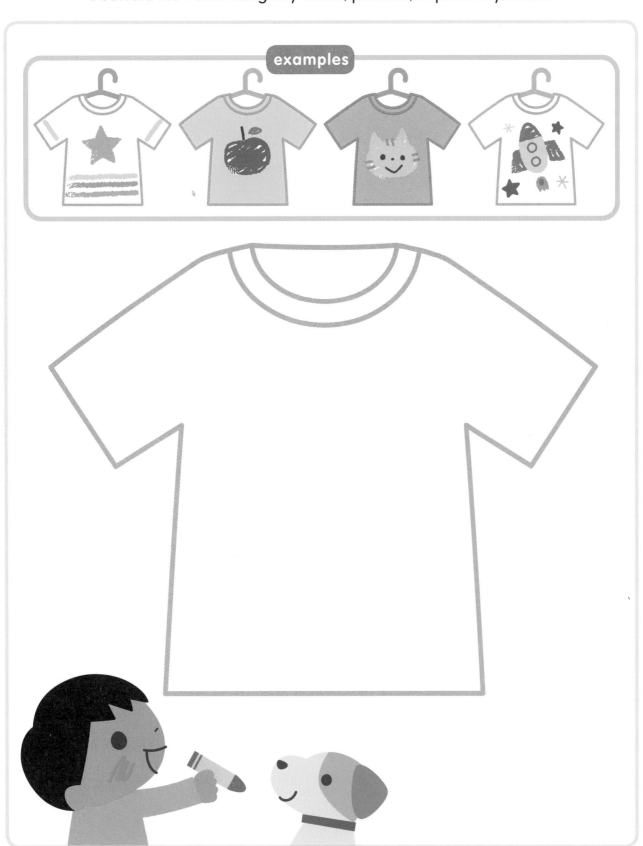

examples

Food Drawing Challenge

Point to and say the name of each food in the example box. Then, draw your favorite on the table.

example

apple   grapes   carrot   cucumber   orange

Beautiful Blooms

Flowers come in different shapes, sizes, and colors.
Draw flowers using any colors or designs you like.

example

On Our Way!

Connect the **RED** dots in order from I to 3. Then, connect the **BLUE** dots in order.
Use the arrows on the dots to help you.

If your child needs help remembering the order of the numbers, let them refer to the numbers at the bottom of the pages.

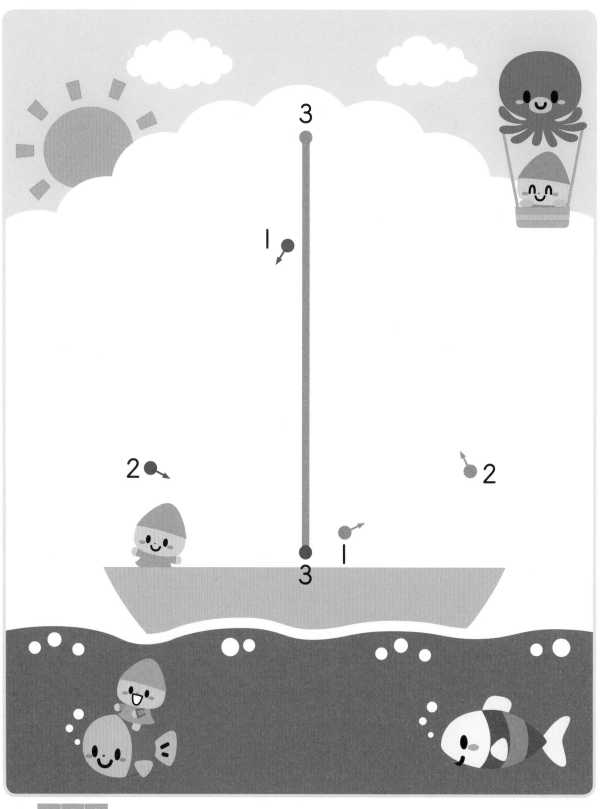

I 2 3

DOT TO DOT

Let It Shine

Connect the **RED** dots in order from 1 to 4. Then, connect the **BLUE** dots in order.
What shapes did you draw?

Puppy Palace

Connect the dots in order from 1 to 5. Use the arrows on the dots to help you.
What do you see?

1 2 3 4 5

DOT TO DOT

Cheep, Cheep!

Connect the **RED** dots in order from 1 to 5.
Then, connect the **BLUE** dots in order from 1 to 5.

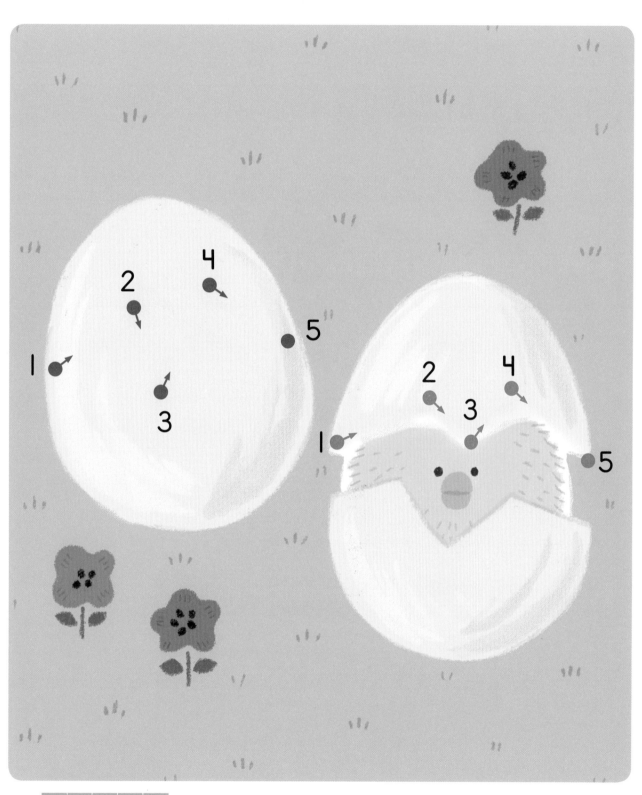

1 2 3 4 5

Strawberry Shortcake

Connect the **RED** dots in order from I to 5.
Then, connect the **BLUE** dots in order from I to 5.

DOT TO DOT

Draw the Swimmer

Connect the dots in order from 1 to 5. What animal do you see?

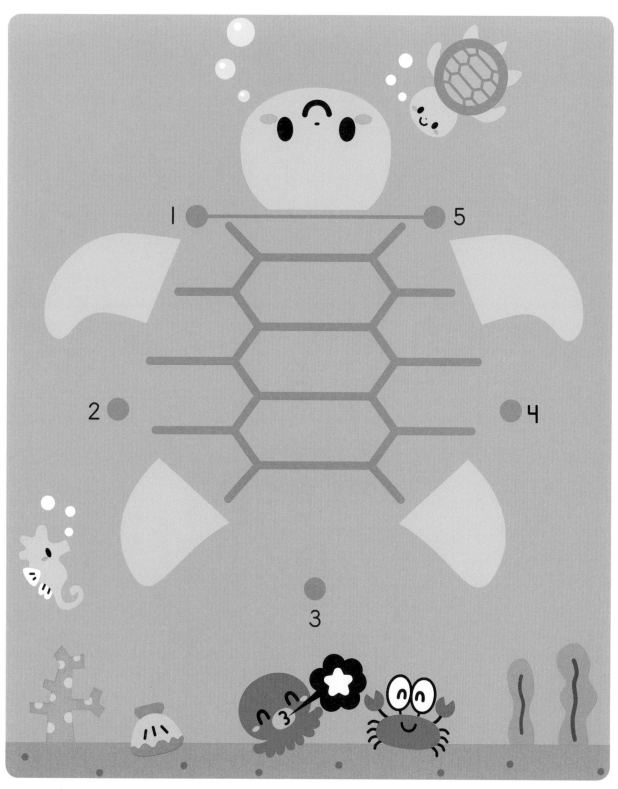

Fantastic Fins

Connect the numbers that are the same. Start by drawing a line between I and I.
What animal do you see?

1 2 3 4 5

Pig Pals

Connect the dots in order from 1 to 6. Use the arrows on the dots to help you.
What noise does this animal make?

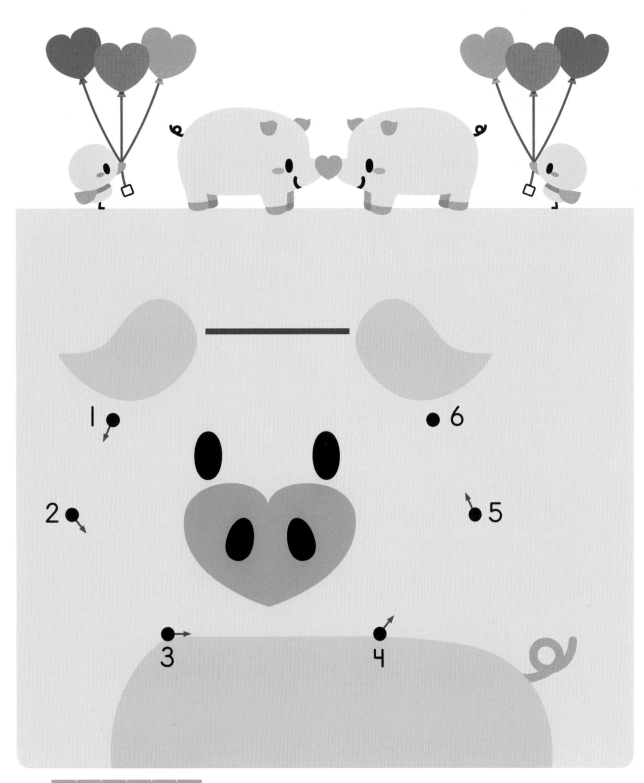

1 2 3 4 5 6

Busy Street

Connect the dots in order from 1 to 6. Look at the number line at the bottom of the page if you need help. Describe the picture.

Rain, Rain, Go Away

Connect the dots in order from 1 to 7.
What do you see?

Dressed and Ready

Connect the dots in order from 1 to 7. Draw the lines as straight as you can.
What is the bear wearing?

DOT TO DOT

Spring Is in the Air

Connect the **BLUE** dots in order from I to 7. Then, connect the **RED** dots in order from I to 7. What insect is flying above the flowers?

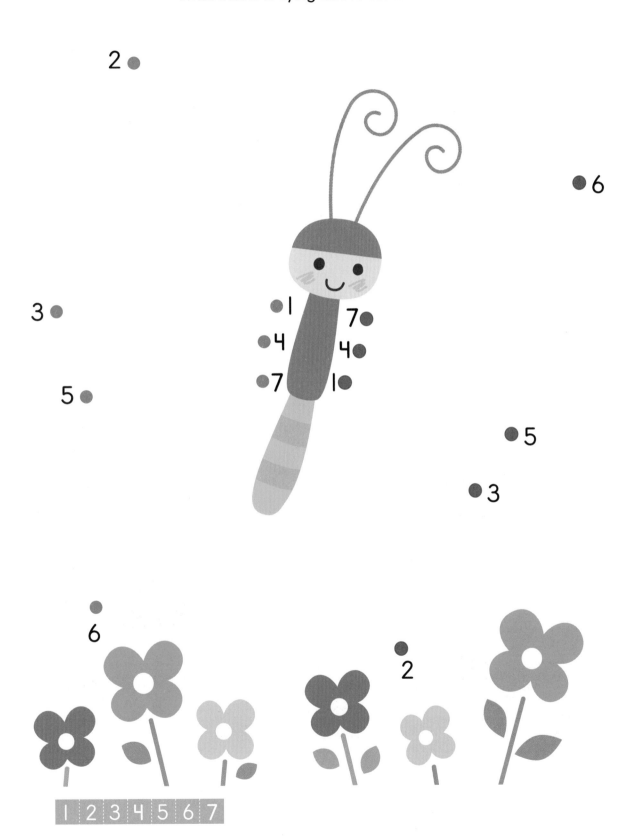

2

6

3

1
7

4
4

7
1

5

3

5

6

2

1 2 3 4 5 6 7

Home, Sweet Home

Connect the dots in order from 1 to 8. Say each number out loud as you go.
What do you see?

Fruit Salad

Connect the dots in order from 1 to 8.
What fruit did you draw?

1 2 3 4 5 6 7 8

An Activity Fit for a King

Connect the dots in order from I to 8. What do you see?

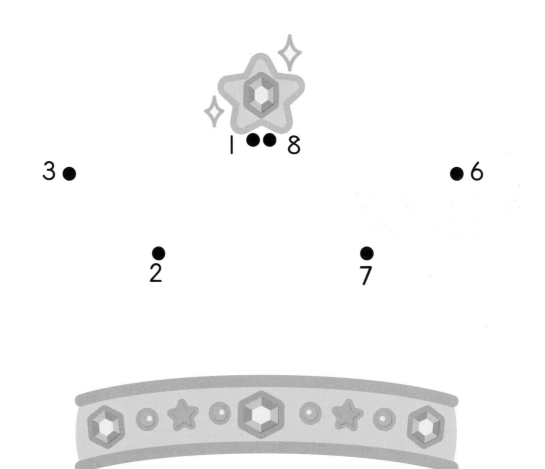

3 ●   I ●● 8   ● 6

●
2   ●
7

4 ●   ● 5

I 2 3 4 5 6 7 8

Sweetly Swinging

Connect the numbers that are the same.
Start by drawing a line between 1 and 1.

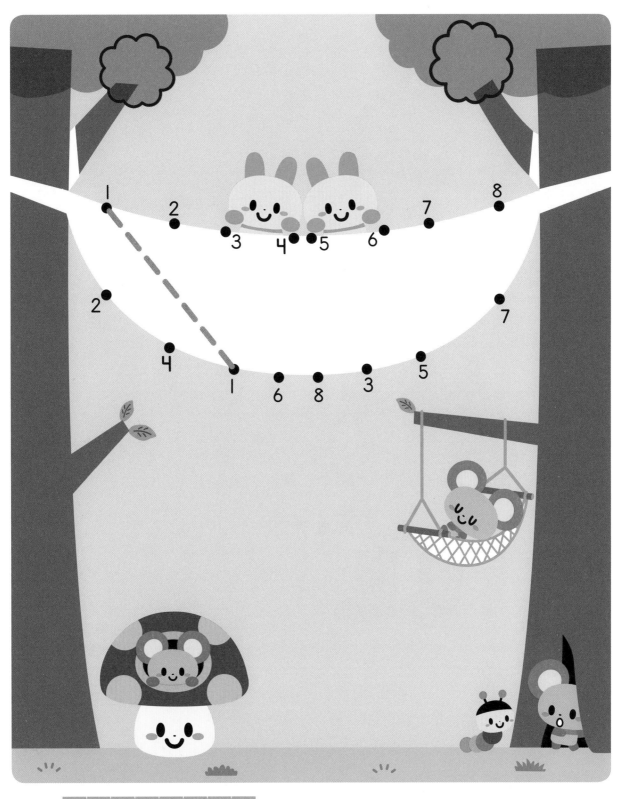

1 2 3 4 5 6 7 8

Splish-Splash!

Connect the dots in order from 1 to 9. Say each number out loud as you go.
What did you draw? Do you like to play in the rain?

DOT TO DOT

Howdy, Partner

Connect the dots in order from 1 to 9.
What did you draw?

In the Clouds

Connect the dots in order from 1 to 9.
What do you see?

DOT TO DOT

Help Mouse Get Home

Connect the dots in order from 1 to 9. Which way should Mouse go?
Say "Go that way!" and point Mouse in the right direction.

Blown Away

Connect the dots in order from 1 to 9.
What is swimming in the sea?

1 2 3 4 5 6 7 8 9

Jack-in-the-Box

Connect the dots in order from I to IO.

Is It Lunchtime Yet?

Connect the dots in order from 1 to 10. Say each number out loud as you go.
What did you draw?

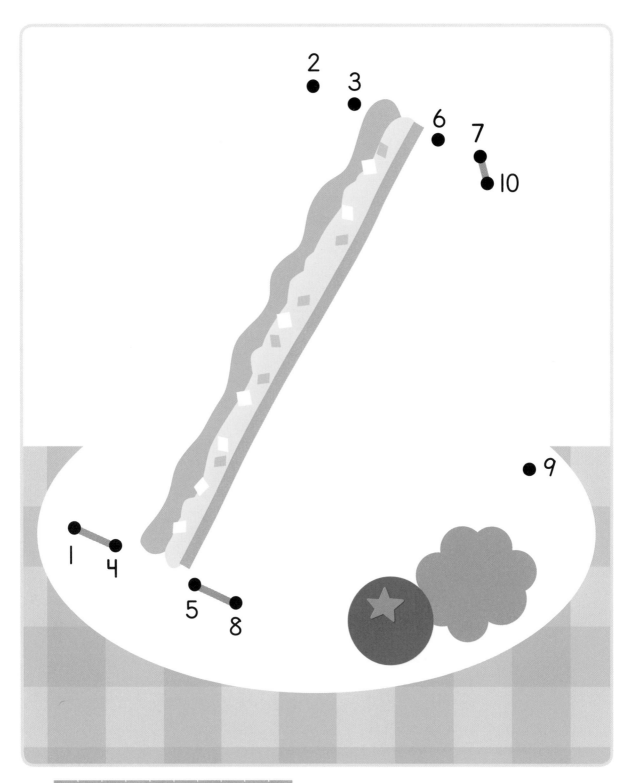

DOT TO DOT

Find the Numbered Dots

Connect the dots in order from 1 to 10. Watch out for the dots that don't have numbers. What did you draw?

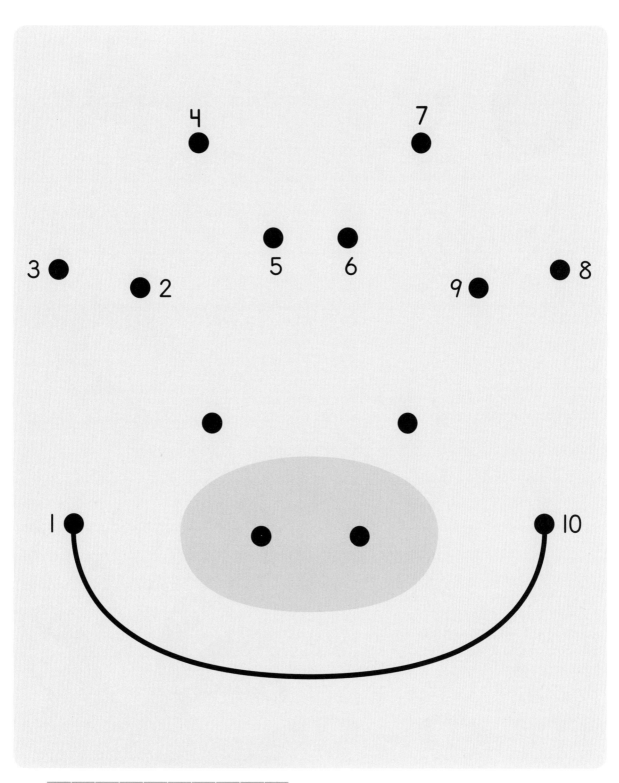

Jumping for Joy

Connect the dots in order from 1 to 10.
What animal did you draw? What is it doing?

1 2 3 4 5 6 7 8 9 10

Next Stop: The Playground!

Connect the dots in order from 1 to 10 to create a path.
Then, draw a line from ➡ to ➡ to help the bear get to the playground.

Wildlife Walk

Start by drawing a line between 5 and 5. Then, connect all the numbers that are the same. Draw a line from ➡ to ➡ to show the mouse a path through the woods.

| 1 | 2 | 3 | 4 | 5 | 6 | 7 | 8 | 9 | 10 |

DOT TO DOT

Draw a Furry Friend

Connect the **BLUE** dots in order from 1 to 10. Then, connect the **RED** dots in order from 1 to 10. What sound does this animal make?

Polar Playtime

Connect the **RED** dots in order from 1 to 10. Connect the **GREEN** dots in order from 1 to 10.
Then, connect the **BLUE** dots in order from 1 to 10.
What do you see?

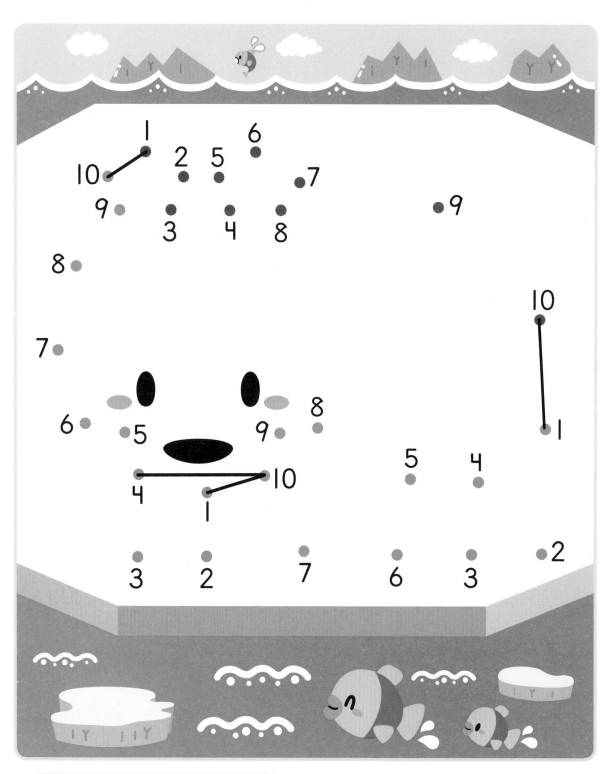

DOT TO DOT

A Winter Wonder

Connect the dots in order from 1 to 11.
Look at the number line at the bottom of the page if you need help.

1 2 3 4 5 6 7 8 9 10 11

3-2-1 Blastoff!

Connect the dots in order from 1 to 11. Say each number out loud as you go. What do you see?

DOT TO DOT

I See You!

Connect the dots in order from 1 to 12.
What did you draw?

Catch Me If You Can

Connect the dots in order from 1 to 12. Say each number out loud as you go. What is the boy doing?

1 2 3 4 5 6 7 8 9 10 11 12

Tending the Garden

Connect the dots in order from 1 to 12. Say each number out loud as you go.
What is the bunny doing?

Hop, Hop, Hopping Along

Connect the dots in order from 1 to 12.
What did you draw?

DOT TO DOT

Race to the Top of the Hill

Show two kids the way to the top of the hill. First use your finger to trace a line from ➡ to ➡ . Then, draw a line from ➡ to ➡ .

Help the Potato Farmer

Help the farmer bring his potatoes to the farm.
First use your finger to trace a line from ➡ to ➡.
Then, draw a line from ➡ to ➡.

MAZES

Make a Wish!

Draw a line from ➡ to ➡ to go through the cake.
Then, pretend to blow out the candles!

Take the Tiger Challenge!

Draw a line from ➡ to ➡ to go through the tiger maze.

MAZES

Splish-Splash

Draw a line from ➡ to ➡ to find a path through the bubbles.

Which Is Which?

The yarn is all tangled up! Use a matching marker or crayon to color one path **RED** and the other path **BLUE**.

Take a Stroll with Mouse

Follow the path from ➡ to ➡ to go to Mouse's house.

Rabbit's Garden Stroll

Draw a path through the maze from ➡ to ➡.
Watch out for the spiderweb!

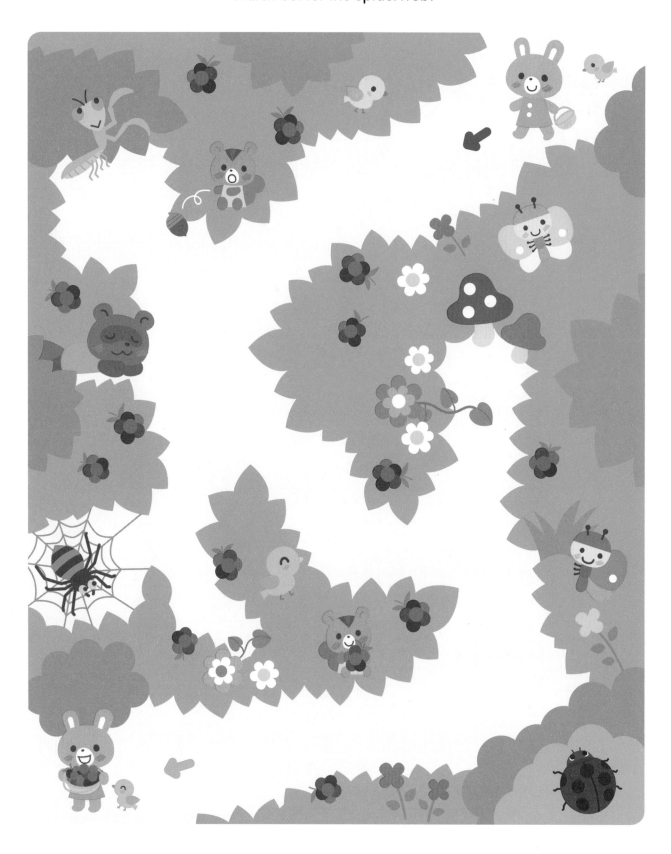

MAZES

Batter Up!

Draw a line from ➡ to ➡ to go through the baseball cap.
There are lots of turning points. It's okay to stop completely before changing directions.

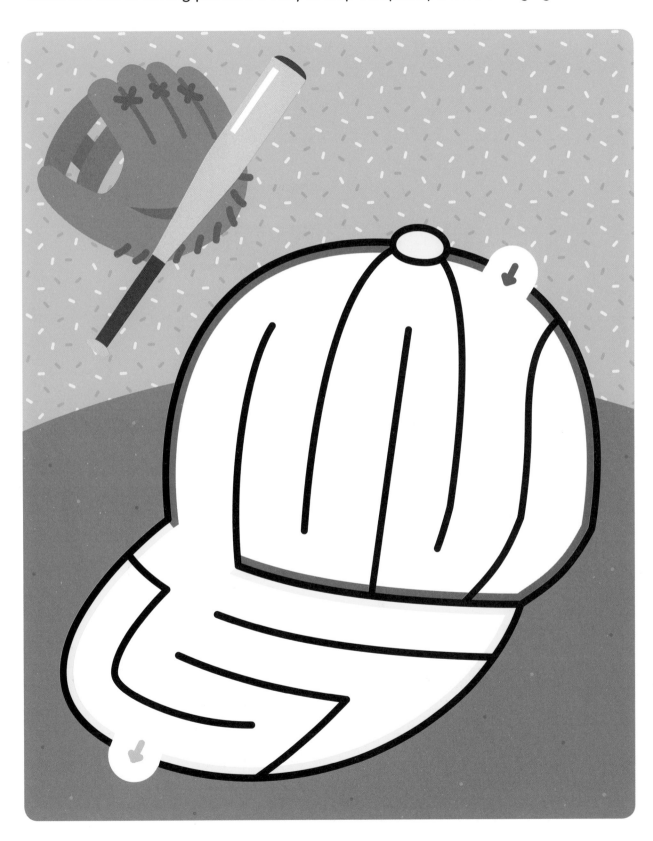

All Aboard!

Draw a line from ➡ to ➡. Try not to get stuck in any dead ends!

Soccer Practice

Draw a line from ➡ to ➡ to go through the soccer ball.
Try not to draw over any of the **BLACK** lines.

Follow the Strings

Trace the dotted lines from ➡ to ➡.
Which line is connected to the rabbit balloon?

Let's Go for a Walk

Trace the dotted lines from ➡ to ➡.
Which line leads to the pig?

Undersea Maze

Draw a line from ➡ to ➡. What animal do you see?

Fruity Maze

Draw a line from ➡ to ➡ to go through the watermelon.

Swirly Snail Maze

Draw a line from ➡ to ➡. When you are done, say "snail shell."

Mystery Maze

Draw a line from ➡ to ➡. What do you see?

Tabletop Maze

Draw a line from ➡ to ➡. What utensils do you use to eat dinner? Which utensil do you see?

MAZES

Yarn Maze

Draw a line from ➡ to ➡ to find a path through the yarn.

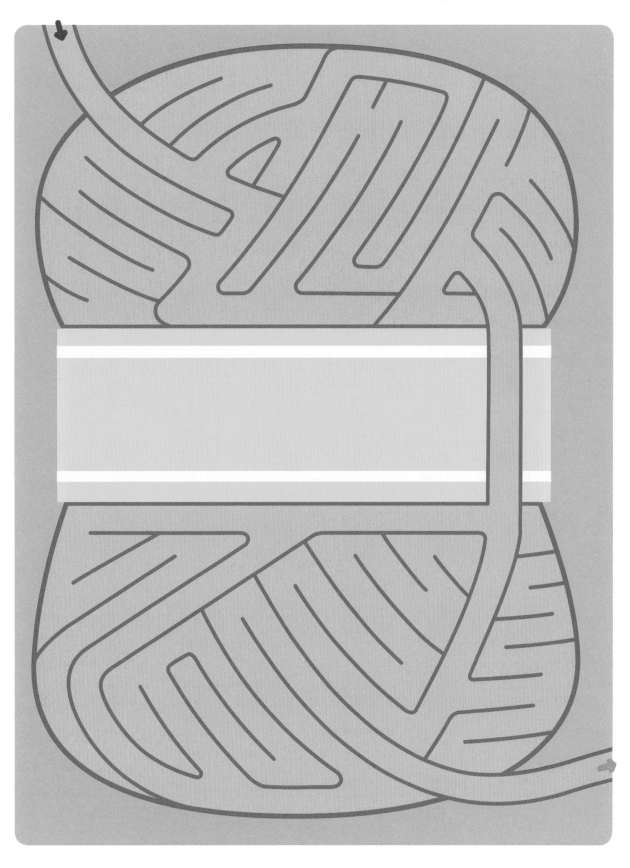

Spot the Mystery Animal

Color the path from ➡ to ➡. Try to stay within the white path.
What shape do you see?

Uncover a Secret Shape!

Color the path from ➡ to ➡. Try to stay within the white path.
What shape do you see?

Reveal a Hidden Picture

Color the path from ➡ to ➡. Try to stay within the white path.
What shape do you see?

MAZES

Kitchen Challenge

Draw a line from ➡ to ➡.
As you pass through each utensil, say what it is.

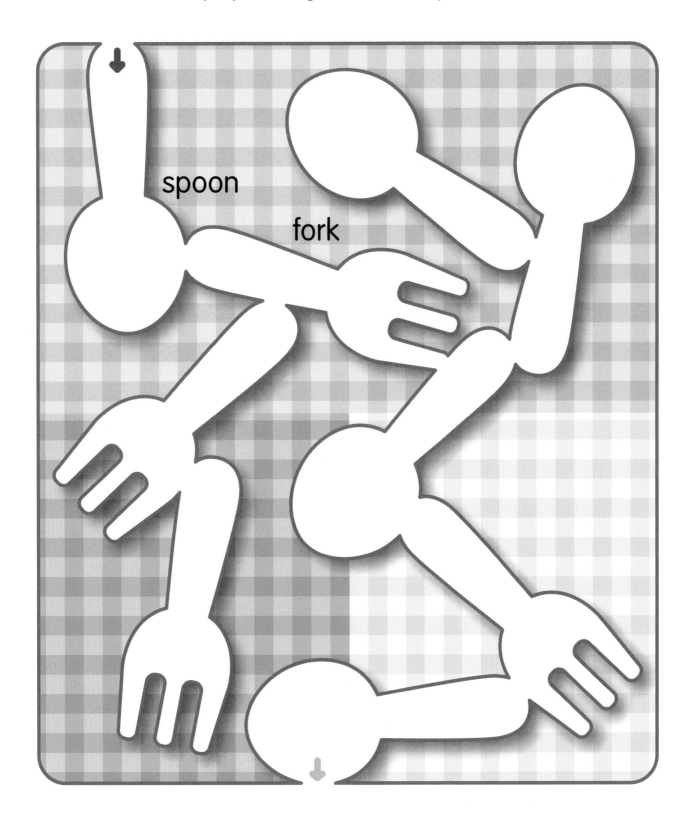

spoon

fork

Monkey's Island Getaway

Draw a line from ➡ to ➡ to help Monkey fly through the clouds to get to the island.

Let's Go Out for Lunch

Draw a line from ➡ to ➡ to show the bears the way to the restaurant.
Say "hi" to the cats on the way.

Where Does Ant Live?

Draw a line from ➡ to ➡ to see how Ant gets back home.
Stop at each intersection and decide which way to go.
Doing mazes like this helps you learn to think ahead.

MAZES

River Safari

Take a ride down the river to get to the ocean.
Draw a line from ➡ to ➡.
Say the names of the animals you pass along the way.

Penguin's Icy Adventure

Help Penguin get to her friends. Draw a path through the maze from ➡ to ➡.

Find the Petal Path

Draw a line through the petals from ➡ to ➡.

Let's Go for a Ride!

Draw a line from ➡ to ➡ to get to the amusement park. What is your favorite ride?

Let's Party!

Draw a line from ➡ to ➡ to help the boy deliver the cake to the party.

Cinderella's Carriage Ride

Draw a line from ➡ to ➡ to help Cinderella get to the castle.

MAZES

Jack's Path Through the Beanstalk

Draw a line from ➡ to ➡ to find out which path will take Jack to the Giant's castle in the sky.

Find a Path Through the Castle!

Draw a line from ➡ to ➡ to find out which path leads through the castle.

Collect the Cheese!

Draw a line from ➡ to ➡. Take the path with only triangle-shaped cheeses.

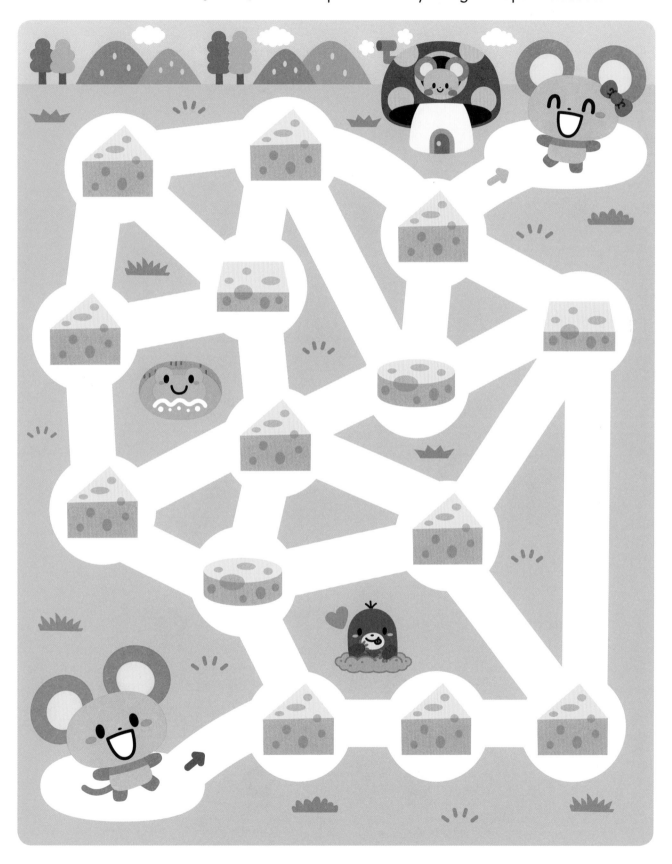

Follow the Flowers

Bee is delivering honey to a friend. Show him the way!
Draw a line from ➡ to ➡. Take the path with only **RED** flowers.

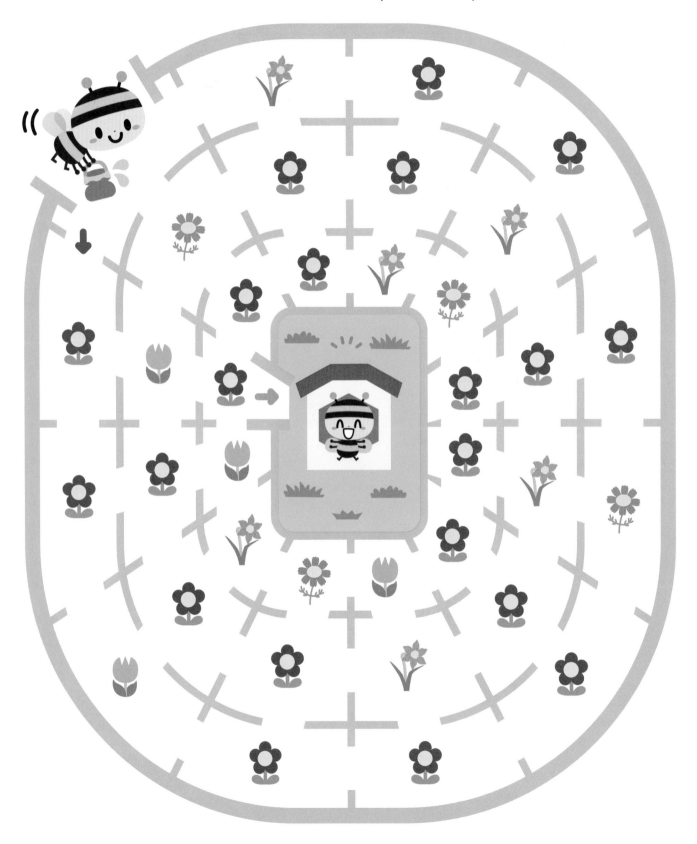

On Your Mark, Get Set, Go!

Draw a line from ➡ to ➡ to get to the finish line and win a prize.
Some of the paths go over or under one another.

Hands Up!

Draw a line from ➡ to ➡. Take the path in the order of 🖐 👣 🖐 👣.
Say the words out loud as you pass over them.

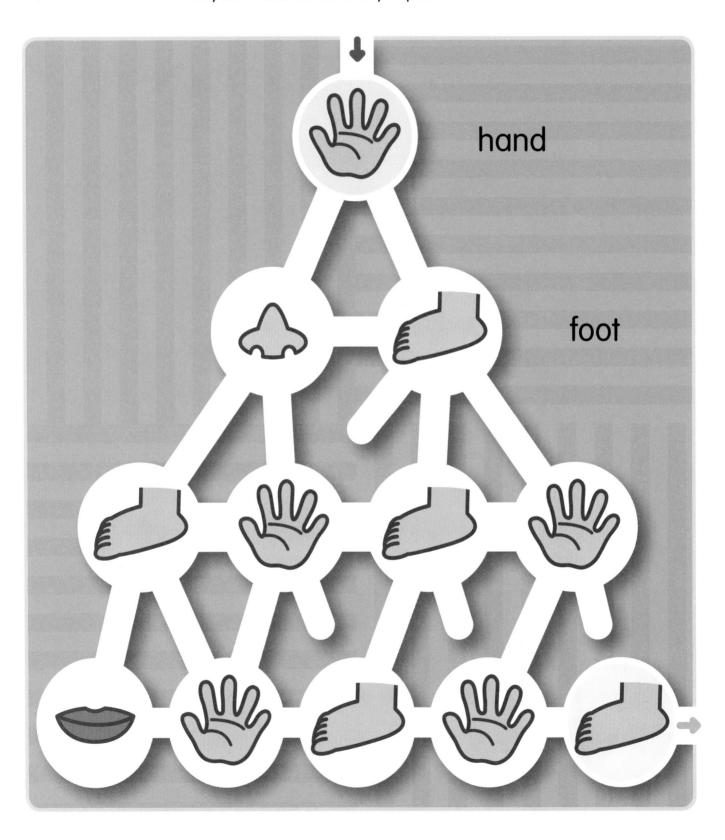

hand

foot

MAZES

Time to Brush Your Teeth

Draw a line from ➡ to ➡. Follow the path that goes
past only things you use when you brush your teeth.

Watch the Flower Grow

Draw a line from ➡ to ➡, following the path that shows how a sunflower grows.
Pass through each picture only once.

MAZES

Treasure Hunter

Draw a line from ➡ to ➡ to help the mouse find the treasure.

Kitchen Helper

Draw a line from ➡ to ➡, following a path of kitchen equipment.

Escape from the Spooky House!

Draw a line from ➡ to ➡ to show the boy the way out of the house.
Take the path with only open doors or ladders.

Strawberry Search

Help Bunny go home. Draw a line from ➡ to ➡. At each split in the path, count the strawberries. Go in the direction of the group that has more strawberries.

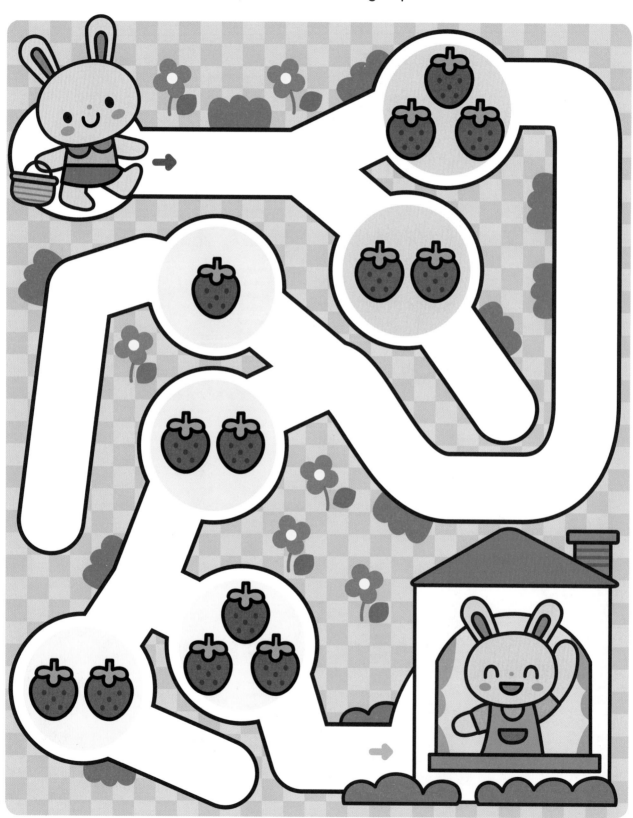

MAZES

Apple Tree Adventure

Draw a line from ➡ to ➡. At each split in the path, count the apples.
Take the path that passes only trees with 3 apples.

Vroooom!

Draw a line from ➡ to ➡ to help Bear drive through the racecourse.
Take the path where the flags go in order of $1 \rightarrow 2 \rightarrow 3 \rightarrow 4 \rightarrow 5$.

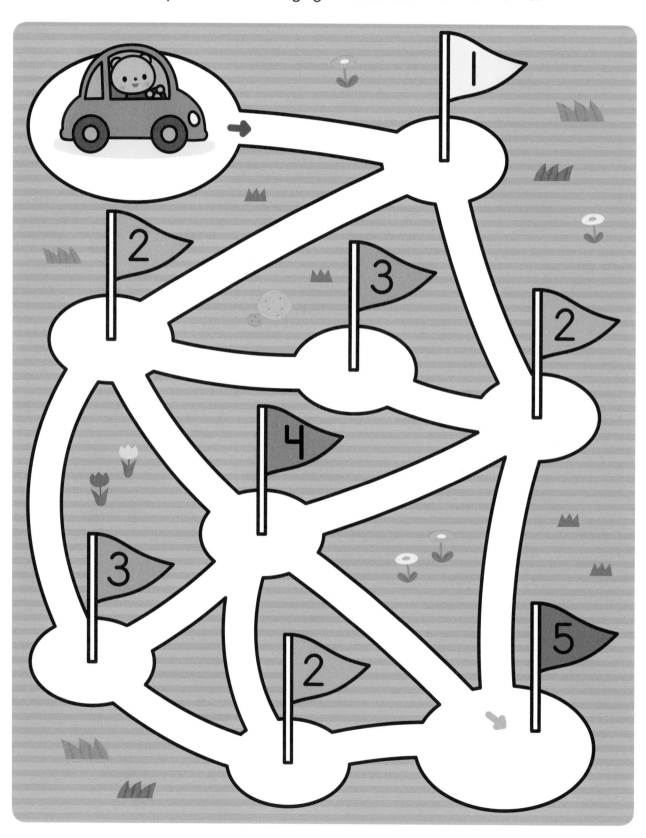

The Acorn Game

Draw a line from → to →. Count each group of acorns as you go.
Take the path in order from 1 to 10 acorns.

Let's Count to 10!

Monkey needs to get to the center of the big top. Draw a line from ➡ to ➡.
Take the path in order of 1→2→3→4→5→6→7→8→9→10.

A-maze-ing Numbers

Draw a line from ➡ to ➡. At each split in the path, count the objects or dots or look at the numbers. Go in the direction of the larger amount or number.

Nature Walk

Draw a line from ➡ to ⮕ by choosing the path with a bigger number.

Find the Treasure

Draw a line from ➡ to ➡. When you have to choose between two paths, count the dots or look at the numbers. Go in the direction of the larger amount or number.

Row, Row, Row the Boat

Help the boy paddle his boat down the river. Draw a line from ➡ to ➡.
When you have to choose between two paths, count the dots or look at the numbers.
Go in the direction of the larger amount or number.

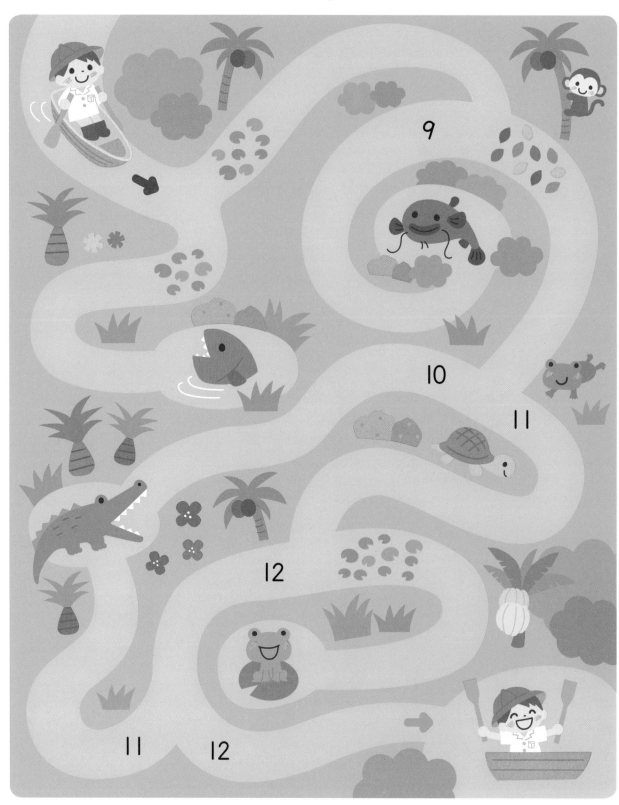

Mail Call

Help the mail carrier deliver the mail.
Draw a line from ➡ to ➡, making sure to go by each house once.

Let's Run Errands

Draw a line from ➡ to ➡. Follow the path that lets you mail a letter, then buy a tomato, then buy a book. Try to use each path only once.

Something Is Fishy

Draw a line from ➡ to ➡ to help the cat pick up all the fish.
You can only take each path once.

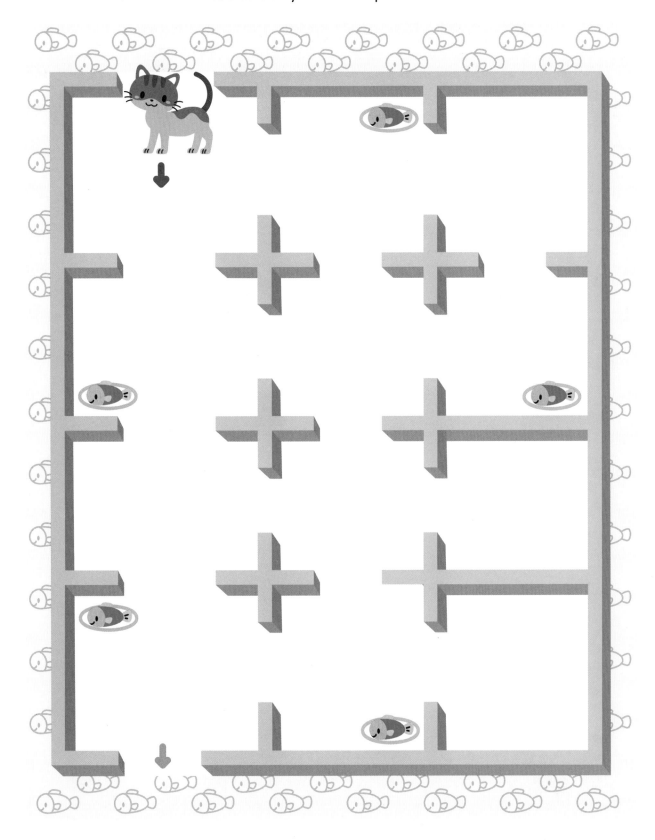

Go Bananas!

Draw a line from ➡ to ➡ to help the monkey collect all the bananas.
You can only take each path once. Watch out for the rocks blocking the way.

Sweet Treats

Draw a path through the maze by following the order  .

Match the Missing Stripes

Oh no! This zebra has lost some of its stripes.
Draw a line to connect the missing pattern in the box to the zebra.

Catch the Matching Fish

Finish drawing each fishing line so it connects to the fish each boy is thinking about.

Find the Rhinoceros

Draw a line from the example picture to the matching shadow.
Then, color the shadow using any color you like.

example

Match the Pattern on the Cow

Draw a line to connect the missing pattern to the cow. When you are done, say "Moo!"

Spot the Shapes

In the picture below, there are 4 ☐, 5 △, and 8 ◯. Find each shape and trace its outline.

Shadow Shuffle

Draw a line from ● to ● to match each animal with its shadow.

Underwater Matching

Find the fish that looks the same as the fish in the example box. Draw a ◯ around it.

PUZZLES

Hide-and-Go-Seek

The animals below are hiding in the picture. Can you help Bear find them? Look closely.
You might only see their ears or their tail. Draw a line from Bear to each of the hidden animals.

Dog   Rabbit   Cat   Mouse

example

Mushroom Match

Trace the shape of the mushrooms below.
Then, draw a line from the mushoom at the top to its matching shape.

Where Is the Koala?

Look at the photograph of the koala at the bottom of the page.
Then, find the exact same koala in the tree. Draw a ◯ around the matching koala.
Make sure it has the same eyes, ears, mouth, and pose.

Let's Make Salad

Which chopped salad below is made from the ingredients in the example picture?
Draw a ◯ around it. Remember: Chopped ingredients look a little different from whole ingredients.

Sandwich Maker

Draw a line from ⬤ to ⬤ to connect the ingredients to the sandwich that is filled with them.

What Is Missing?

Draw a line from each of the ☐ at the bottom of the page
to the ☐ on the giraffe to fill in the picture.

Find the Matching Picture

Look carefully at the shapes of the shadows in the example box.
Find the picture that matches the example and color the ○ using any color you like.

example

High-Flying Match Game

Draw a line from ● to ● to match the helicopters to their tails.